914.241

11849

Gloucestershire Countryside

Access, Exploration
Walks, Nature and Local History

British Library Cataloguing in Publication Data
Ottewell, Gordon
   Gloucestershire Countryside : access, exploration, walks, nature and
   local history.
   1. Walking recreations 2. Gloucestershire (England)
   I. Title
   914.241

   ISBN 1-872454-02-X

Publisher: Minton & Minton, Greylands, Bicton Pool, Kingsland, Nr. Leominster, Herefordshire HR6 9PR. Tel: Yarpole (0568 85) 338.

Typesetter: Impress at Myst, Weobley, Herefordshire.
Typeface: Souvenir 10/11 point, headings 16 point.

Printer: Lambert & Son, Station Road, Settle, North Yorkshire.

Photography: David Minton.

Vignettes: S. G. Minton, Leominster.

Cover: The cover picture is a watercolour of the view above Parks Farm on a track from Salt Way down to Winchcombe, Gloucestershire. Painted by Alec Betterton, Winchcombe, Gloucestershire, it represents typical Gloucestershire countryside on a bright spring day. Alec Betterton, a personal friend of the author, is a retired headmaster whose watercolours are becoming increasingly popular.

Acknowledgements:
I wish to record my appreciation of the help I received from the following people, all of whom gave generously both in time and expertise towards the writing of this book.

Mary Hopkins, who not only typed the manuscripts but also gave invaluable assistance with research and maps.

Hugh Hopkins, who kindly read the manuscript and made many helpful suggestions.

Alec Betterton, who produced the excellent cover picture and kindly loaned useful reference material.

Mr. C. I. Carter, of the Forestry Commission, who gave valuable advice regarding the Forest of Dean.

Finally, Margaret, my wife, who as always gave help and encouragement throughout.

My thanks to all.
Gordon Ottewell

Abbreviations

FC	Forestry Commission	N	North
GCC	Gloucestershire County Council	S	South
GR	Grid Reference	E	East
GTNC	Gloucestershire Trust for Nature Conservation	W	West
NNR	National Nature Reserve		
NT	National Trust		
OL	Outdoor Leisure map		
OS	Ordnance Survey		
RSPB	Royal Society for the Protection of Birds		
SSSI	Site of Special Scientific Interest		
u/c	Unclassified (road)		
WT	Woodland Trust		
⊗	Suitable for pushchair or similar		
	Suitable for walking stick user		

Key to location sketchmaps

━━━━ A road or motorway
───── B road
───── Unclassified road
------- Footpath
P   Parking

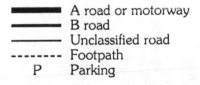 Extent of site (approximate)

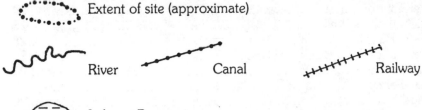

River   Canal   Railway

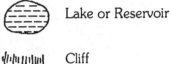 Lake or Reservoir

ḋᵘʰᵘ Cliff

Note:
The publisher and author wish to point out that while every effort has been made to ensure accuracy they cannot be held responsible for location errors or consequences arising from location errors.

Contents

Southern Section

Other information

Foreword

by
Tony Drake, Footpath Secretary Gloucestershire Area,
The Ramblers Association

Most people have an instinctive urge to get out into the countryside and although some are content just to drive through it without stopping, most like to stop, stretch their legs, have a picnic and return home refreshed. For them our wonderful network of public rights of way, despite now being much improved and marked, prove daunting unless they have large scale maps and walk guides. It is the wider open spaces that appeal, where there is freedom to roam at will over commons and attractive woodlands. No book has hitherto sought to give the public a comprehensive guidebook to the accessible countryside of Gloucestershire.

Gordon Ottewell has picked over a hundred special places in Gloucestershire that the public can visit and then explore without difficulty or fear of trespassing – and all except one is for free into the bargain. Special mention is of course given to the extensive and attractive commons along the Cotswold edge, which are amongst the gems of the county's open spaces, as also in a different way, is the Forest of Dean, surely the most attractive forest in Britain. Not quite all the places mentioned are open spaces or woodlands, there being a few linear sites such as canal towpaths and riverside sites which make justifiable inclusions.

Even to those of us who are very familiar with the Gloucestershire countryside, the book makes compelling reading because of the fascinating way the author has brought his wide knowledge of natural history to add to his anecdotes about each place. The reader armed with, at the very least, the Ordnance Survey 1:50,000 Landranger maps to supplement the generalised maps with the text, can look forward to an enjoyable foray for every weekend for the next two years.

1

Introduction

*"The eye must be dim, and the heart benumbed, which
can be insensible to the rural beauty of Gloucestershire."*

These words, written by the agricultural historian William Marshall in
1789, are as true today as they were then. In Marshall's day of course,
travel was a difficult, often hazardous activity restricted to a minority. Most
people seldom ventured beyond their nearest market town and the con-
cept of exploring the countryside for pleasure in the way we do today was
unknown.

Two centuries after Marshall's words of praise, Gloucestershire is recognised as one of England's most popular counties for outdoor leisure pur-
suits. Every year, countless thousands, in car, coach and train, on cycle
and on foot, swell the growing number of local people in seeking out for
themselves the beauty that is Gloucestershire. Many of these visitors, eager
for more, return again and again. Others, convinced that the county possesses just about every quality necessary for a fulfilling life, come here to
live.

Although it is the towns and villages, the parks and historic sites, the fine
houses and beautiful gardens, that lure many to Gloucestershire, the countryside itself provides the setting for these delights. The question of obtaining access to that countryside is one that presents certain difficulties, however. There are plenty of well-used and signposted linear walks, and almost
as many footpath guidebooks of varying quality offering circular walks of
every description. But for those who wish to locate areas of Gloucestershire where they can roam freely, watch wildlife, enjoy a picnic and the
open countryside generally without fear of trespassing, there is no comprehensive publication to give assistance.

The role of this book, therefore, is to encourage country-lovers to discover
the Gloucestershire that other literature fails to reach. It is concerned with
the open spaces of the county — the country parks, commons, greens,
woods, and other areas where the general public is allowed to roam. It also
offers guidance on access to rivers, canals and certain other features that
the seeker after unspoilt countryside may well find enjoyable, even though
they cannot be classified as open spaces in the normal sense of the word.

It should be remembered that all land in Britain is owned by someone. The
owner may be the county council, a body such as the National Trust, or, as
in the case of most open countryside, a private individual or company. Obviously, the greater part of this land is put to use — farming, horticulture
and forestry between them account for almost all of Gloucestershire's open
countryside — but there remain a surprising number of areas to which the
public has rights of access and it is with these, which vary enormously both
in size and character, that we are primarily concerned in this book.

Using the Book

Gloucestershire's rural beauty is largely attributable to its diversity of scenery. One of the county's poets described this as 'Forest, vale and high blue hill', and this apt, if sweeping way of summarising the scenic mix could well serve as a basic framework for this book.

Instead, however, I have decided upon five sections, each encompassing a distinctive region — Wye Valley, Forest of Dean, Over Severn, Severn Vale, and the Cotswolds. Even with this form of division, a few 'grey areas' remain, but at least the groupings may prove useful to those unfamiliar with the topography of the county and to those others for whom some order is essential for a rewarding exploration of a familiar landscape.

The fact that this method of dividing Gloucestershire has led to one region the Cotswolds — offering more locations than all the others combined, in no way implies that the celebrated limestone region enjoys a monopoly of scenic delights. Rather it is an indicator that the Cotswolds are well-blessed with accessible countryside, especially commons, which are sadly lacking in other regions, although in the case of the Forest of Dean, this is more than compensated for by the open-access policy of the Forestry Commission.

Now to the all-important matter of finding the sites. This is tackled in three ways, firstly by means of a county sketchmap, secondly by use of small location sketchmaps, and finally by reference to Ordnance Survey maps.

County Sketchmap: This appears at the back of the book and in addition to showing main routes, contains the positions of all sites, identifiable by their page numbers.

The location sketchmaps: Every site is marked on one of these maps, although to avoid unnecessary duplication, some maps include more than one site. These simple maps show the position of the site in relation to main access roads. The scales are variable depending on the overall size of the area covered by the map and the extent of the site, which may range from a small village green to a vast tract of woodland. The dotted boundaries of the sites are approximate only and should not be taken as indicating necessarily the exact area to which there is public access. In a few cases, especially the Forest of Dean, these limits have been omitted as the parking points give access to extensive unrestricted areas of woodland. Used in conjunction with a good road map, these location sketchmaps should ensure that all sites can be found without any difficulty.

Although not intended for guidance over the sites themselves, some of the location sketchmaps include public footpaths (marked by broken lines) and specific features, such as landmarks and viewpoints.

Ordnance Survey Maps: No meaningful exploration of the Gloucestershire countryside can be carried out without reference to OS maps. Most of the county of covered by the 1:50,000 scale Landranger sheets 162 (Gloucester and Forest of Dean) and 163 (Cheltenham and Cirencester Area), but for complete coverage, it is also necessary to obtain sheets 149 (Hereford, Leominster and surrounding area), 150 (Worcester and the Malverns) and 151 (Stratford-upon-Avon). For a detailed exploration of the west of the county, the large-scale (1:25,000) Outdoor Leisure 14 (Wye Valley and Forest of Dean) is an excellent investment.

The sheet number of the relevant Landranger map (together with Outdoor Leisure 14 where appropriate) is given at the head of every site description. This is followed by the OS Grid Reference (GR) using the numbered grid lines on the map to pinpoint the main access point (or other specified location) to the nearest one hundred metres. Full instructions for using grid references are given on Landranger maps; the only difference in this book is that the easting (the first three figures obtained from the lines runnning north to south) is separated from the northing (second three figures obtained from the lines running east to west) by an oblique stroke (/) to make reading the numbers easier.

Parking: Although a good number of the sites included are on or near bus routes, rural service are so limited and changeable that it seems realistic to suppose that most readers will travel by car. With this in mind, a few words of advice are given on parking. Many sites have good parking facilities, at others this is limited, while occasionally, there is no on-site parking and vehicles must be left in nearby lanes. Please remember in such cases to leave plenty of space for wide farm vehicles to pass and avoid blocking gateways.

Nature of terrain: The section in heavy print at the head of each route description concludes with a brief summary of the nature of the terrain, the types of tracks or paths, seasonal conditions, and details, if applicable, of the extent and ownership of the site. Many locations offer a range of options from gentle strolls along level sward to challenging climbs over rough ground. In some places, the going underfoot varies greatly depending on the season. Bearing in mind the fickle nature of the British climate, it is a wise maxim to take too much, rather than too little warm and weather-resistant clothing, and to pay particular attention to footwear — the sturdier the better at all times!

A word about the suitablility or otherwise of sites for pushchairs, wheelchairs and less-able walkers. As a general rule, locations described as flat, or offering easy walking, should prove accessible in most cases, except occasionally when a public footpath crosses stiles. Speed the day when more fine hilltop sites are equipped, as is Dover's Hill, with special wheelchair gates and tracks.

Site description: Over a hundred different sites are described in the five sections of this book. Though by no means exhaustive, they are county-wide in extent and range from small village greens and wayside commons, to larger expanses of open country and, in the case of the Forest of Dean, to a carefully selected number of starting points for exploring a vast area to which we, the public, have virtually unrestricted acccess.

By contrast, I have also included several sites of exceptional merit which are privately owned and in which walking is restricted to public footpaths only. These are indicated by the word 'private' in the summary in heavy type at the head of the site description. Without exception, the public rights-of-way over these sites were clearly way-marked at the time the book was researched amd walkers should experience no difficulty in finding their way. However, it should be borne in mind that public footpaths provide linear access only over private ground and that there is no automatic right to picnic or to deviate from these rights-of-way. Please, therefore, respect all boundary fences and do not stray onto surrounding private land.

The descriptions of individual sites are in no way intended to be definitive. They are merely an attempt to provide the reader with some idea of what to expect and are therefore written in general terms. Consequently, themes range widely over such subjects as geology, archaeology, history and natural history. Readers with specialist interests will no doubt discover a great deal more on their visit than can possibly be included here.

A number of the locations are Sites of Special Scientific Interest (SSSIs) or nature reserves, while others are of important archaeological and/or historical value. The utmost care should be taken in such places not to cause damage or disturbance. Each is a precious part of our Gloucestershire heritage. Cherish it!

The countryside — caring and sharing: The Gloucestershire countryside is ours to share. Whether we choose to follow a long-distance footpath, climb a rugged hilltop, stroll along a bridleway or snooze in the shade of an ancient oak, we are deriving pleasure from some aspect of this richly varied landscape.

Sharing these delights, as we are free to do in these and countless other ways, demands of us a caring concern in return. In the words of a notice seen by the roadside near Snowshill:
*'Let no-one say and say it to your shame
that all was beauty here until you came.'*

Sadly, as can be seen all too often at some of the sites described here, the Country Code still falls on deaf ears. Litter and vandalism, thoughtlessness and discourtesy are all too evident in the heart of rural Gloucestershire today.

It is said, in truth, that the countryside needs all the friends it can get. Hopefully, this book will win more friends for our beautiful county —sharers in its delights and carers who honour the Country Code:

THE COUNTRY CODE

GUARD AGAINST ALL RISK OF FIRE.

FASTEN ALL GATES.

KEEP DOGS UNDER PROPER CONTROL.

KEEP TO PATHS ACROSS FARMLAND.

AVOID DAMAGING FENCES, HEDGES AND WALLS.

LEAVE NO LITTER.

SAFEGUARD WATER SUPPLIES.

PROTECT WILDLIFE PLANTS & TREES.

GO CAREFULLY ON COUNTRY ROADS.

RESPECT THE LIFE OF THE COUNTRYSIDE.

Enjoy your exploration of the Gloucestershire countryside!

The Wye Valley

Gloucestershire is fortunate in having a generous share of the lower Wye Valley — some 30 meandering miles — which partially forms its western boundary. It shares this beautiful scenic region with Herefordshire and Gwent (formerly Monmouthshire) and although the actual boundary leaves the river in places, the landscape never loses its distinctive Wye Valley character.

Gloucestershire initially lays claim to the Wye's eastern bank near Marstow, between Ruardean and Goodrich. Lower Lydbrook is the county's first and only river-bank village before the Wye carves its dramatic horseshoe loop into Herefordshire round the Huntsham peninsula. Although most of Symonds Yat lies outside Gloucestershire, the famous Yat Rock itself belongs to the county and is one of its major attractions.

South of Symonds Yat, the Wye serves as the county boundary for a mere mile before Gloucestershire parts company with the river in the Monmouth area, only to meet up once more at Redbrook, an association which continues southwards now for the remainder of the Wye's course, as far as its confluence with the Severn close by the Severn Bridge at Beachley.

The Wye has long been considered one of Britain's most beautiful rivers. It has already covered the greater part of its scenically magnificent course on its seaward journey from Mount Plynlimon by the time it reaches Gloucestershire, but it keeps a few delights for its later stages. These include dramatic rock outcrops and extensive ancient woodland, together with a rich population of plant and animal life. The lower reaches of the river are affected by the tides which carry saltwater as far upstream as Brockweir. Tidal variation in water depth extends even further, reaching Bigsweir Bridge. All this adds to the value of the Wye Valley as a region of outstanding natural beauty and although space permits the inclusion of only a few sites particularly worth exploring, readers will have no difficulty in discovering many more on their own — always an extremely satisfying experience.

Also included in this section are certain wooded areas to the south of the Forest of Dean. These, although not strictly within the Wye Valley, are so close to the region that a visitor might wish to explore some of them in conjunction with the Valley itself.

Lancaut

Maps 162 and OL 14, GR 542/967.
Parking: On verge, 250 yds along Lancaut Lane, signposted off B4228, half-a-mile N of Woodcroft.

Public footpath through private woodland, riverbank and quarries. Some steep climbs and muddy patches unavoidable.

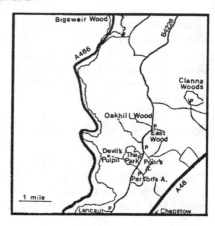

Few days out in Gloucestershire can compare with this. A visit to Lancaut combines exceptional woodland walking with a stretch of spectacular scenery along the east bank of the Wye Gorge, plus—for those who can take rough scrambling and steep slopes in their stride—a dramatic ascent by sheer quarry faces to reach the Offa's Dyke Path near Wintour's Leap. Add to all this a visit to the romantic ruin of a tiny church crumbling close to the water's edge and you have almost a surfeit of good things packed into a single location—something of a feat in itself.

From the car park, enter the woods along a waymarked footpath in about 200 yards, which descends to the left just after Lancaut Lane begins to dip. The path is clear and passes tiny cells hollowed out of the rocks on the right before forking left to cross a metal stile.

Lancaut Woods are both dark and deep with ancient yews creating an atmosphere of sombre majesty, and ferny hollows providing their own distinctive air of mystery. Interspersed with these are veteran oaks and beeches, patches of hazel and a few stout hornbeams towering on fluted trunks above the lower vegetation. Here, in summer, nuthatches whistle boldly and the low drone of unseen myriads of flies accompanies every step.

Beyond the next stile, the path swings to the left and the woods change character. A broken canopy, comprising old ashes and birches, dominates a varied understorey of hawthorn and field maple, succeeded in turn by extensive patches of old hazel coppice.

Perched on a slope above the looping Wye, hemmed in by woodland, St. James's church is a roofless ruin, with bracken doing its best to obliterate the few pathetic gravestones dotted about what remains of the churchyard.

The Norman font was long ago taken for safety to Gloucester Cathedral, leaving a battered shell miraculously retaining a little of its dignity despite years of neglect and exposure to the elements.

From the church, the intrepid can follow the Wye for some distance as it sweeps in a vast arc downstream, bound for Chepstow and its meeting with the Severn. Ahead, great grey cliffs tower 250 feet above the river, echoing at weekends with the voices of climbers calling to one another from ledge to ledge on the sheer rock face high above. These cliffs also provide nesting sites for ravens whose deep throated croaks mingle with the human sounds.

This stretch of the walk incorporates a glimpse of salt-marsh flora, which in occurring cheek by jowl with valley woodland, give rise to a combination of habitat rarely found in Britain. Depending on the state of the tide, banks of sticky mud may be exposed, at the edge of which two plants in particular are worth noting. One is sea aster, a close relative of the ubiquitous michaelmas daisy, and the other, the fleshy ground-hugging English scurvygrass with its distinctive sprays of small white flowers.

Between this muddy zone and the path, is a strip of salt-marsh proper, populated by a range of specialist plants guaranteed to gladden a botanist's eye. These include two plantains—sea and buck's-horn, and sea spurrey and sea milkwort.

It is hardly surprising therefore that the footpath eventually foresakes the shoreline and climbs into the woods before joining the Offa's Dyke Path south of Wintour's Leap.

The gradually ascending woodland path holds further treats in store for the naturalist. Here, regenerating wild service trees abound, together with yew, whitebeam and small-leaved lime. Wild privet and spurge laurel are well established in the quarries, and rock faces shelter red valerian, calamint, centaury, yellow-wort and marjoram, and their associated insect life—butterflies, moths and bees.

Back on the B4228 after striking the Offa's Dyke Path, there remains one further experience to savour—for those with a head for heights—Wintour's Leap. This spot—supposedly from where Royalist Sir John Wintour leaped to escape the pursuing Parliamentarians in 1642—is now merely a gap between houses by the side of the busy road, but the view is— quite literally—breathtaking.

Tidenham Chase

The name Tidenham Chase conjures up impressions of an ancient hunting forest, which is exactly what covered much of this part of south Gloucestershire — the land between the Wye and the Severn — in bygone times. It was the preserve of the Lords of Striguil and although near to the Forest of Dean, was not considered as belonging to it.

Such was the vastness of the Chase that as recently as the mid-fifteenth century, its wolves were considered so hazardous to the people of the locality that the vicar of Tidenham was allowed to leave the village for fear of them.

Apart from the name on a map, the Chase has long since gone. In its place are a few scattered patches of woodland, most of which are under the care of the Forestry Commission. Of these, the most accessible and rewarding are The Park (with its optional walk to the Devil's Pulpit), Poor's Allotment and Parson's Allotment.

The Park

**Maps 162 and OL 14, GR 559/993.   Location sketchmap see page 8.
Parking: Car park, 3.5 miles S of St. Briavels on B4228.**

FC woodland with wide, easy tracks. Optional linear walk of approximately 1 mile to Devil's Pulpit, well signposted across fields. Excellent views over Wye Valley.

Although consisting primarily of conifer plantations, The Park also contains a range of heathland plants - relics of the ground vegetation of the old Chase. These include heather, bell heather and bilberry which, together with patches of gorse and such flowering plants as centaury, tormentil and hemp agrimony, provide plenty of interest along the rides.

Nor do the conifers have it all their own way as far as the trees are concerned, for rowan and birch are well established and a scatter of whitebeam provides further variety.

Those wishing to extend their woodland wander to include a visit to the Devil's Pulpit, about a mile distant, should keep left at the triangulation pillar at a meeting of rides in the centre of the wood. On reaching the quaintly-named Miss Grace's Lane, turn right along it, and in 300 yards left to cross a stile into the fields. From here, the path is clearly way-marked.

The Devil's Pulpit is a rocky outcrop overlooking the Wye Valley, with a superb view of Tintern Abbey below. It is said to have got its name from having been used by Old Nick as a vantage point from where he tried, without success, to tempt the monks of Tintern to renounce their vows and follow him.

Alongside Offa's Dyke Path close by, can be seen the floor of an old quarry in which a veteran yew tree has put down roots deep into the bedrock.

Poor's Allotment Viewpoint ⊕

Parking: As for The Park.

Short walk from car park to rocky outcrop overlooking Severn Vale.

Back at the car park, cross the road and pass through a kissing gate into Poor's Allotment. A short walk leads to another rocky outcrop, this time offering a panorama of the Severn — the Sharpness Docks complex dominating to the north, the nuclear power stations of Berkeley and Oldbury prominent ahead, and the bold outline of the Severn

Bridge away to the south.

According to legend, the Devil was also once active here, challenging a mythical local strong man, Jack Kent, to a stone-throwing contest. Taking first go, Old Nick pitched his stone a mere mile-and-a-half, to where it can now be seen on the bank of the Severn as the Broad Stone, near Stroat. Not to be outdone, brave Jack hurled his stone right across the Severn, but there is some argument concerning the exact spot at which it fell.

Parson's Allotment

Maps 162 and OL 14, GR 561/985. Location sketchmap see page 8.
Parking: By entrance to forest ride, half-a-mile down u/c road (Rosemary Lane) off B4228, 4 miles S of St. Briavels.

Easy walking over FC land. Stone

monolith and good views of Severn estuary.

This is the southernmost tract of woodland in the Tidenham area. It is separated from Poor's Allotment by Rosemary Lane, which wriggles its tortuous way between the two main roads referred to above.

11

The wood gets its name from having been the property of the vicars of Tidenham, whose poor parishioners had their rights of pasturage in the adjoining Poor's Allotment, already mentioned.

On the south-east of Parson's Allotment stands the Jubilee Stone, so called on account of the inscription 'VR 1837 — 1897' cut into its rough surface. This slender, ten-foot-high monument, with its jagged, tapering profile is obviously very much older than its name suggests.

Much of this wood has been clear-felled and recently replanted with conifers. Until these grow, there are excellent views of the Severn through patches of birch scrub. Heather and gorse add colour and character to this remnant of the Chase nearest to the village to which it owes its name.

East Wood ⊕

Maps 162 and OL14, GRs 559/003 (south) and 564/008 (north). Location sketchmap — see page 8.
Parking: South — Near entrance of FC ride at south end of wood, off B4228, 3 miles S of St. Briavels. North — Lay-by, 2.5 miles S of St. Briavels on B4228.

Level woodland terrain with easy walking. Small limestone pavements rough underfoot and partly obscured by summer vegetation.

Together with Oakhill Wood, opposite across the B4228, East Wood comprises one of the largest tracts of woodland on the southern fringe of the Forest of Dean. The northern sections of these woods can best be explored from the layby at GR 564/008, but the southern part of East Wood is especially interesting for two features — limestone pavements and a venerable old yew tree.

The two small areas of limestone pavement are situated on either side of the woodland ride. They are about 200 yards apart and connected by paths. Blue posts mark their position. They comprise the sole remnants of weathered outcrops of Carboniferous Drybrook Limestone, others having long since been lost from view beneath plantings of trees.

Though on a much smaller scale than those of Malham on the Yorkshire Pennines, these pavements display a similar clint-and-grike structure, with the deep narrow grooves worn between the bleached limestone rocks providing ideal habitat for a variety of flowering plants as well as two distinctive ferns, the strap-shaped hart's tongue and the small, delicate black spleenwort. The Gloucestershire Trust for Nature

Conservation is responsible for the management of these pavements. This entails stemming the encroachment of scrub and coppice regrowth, and cutting back the brambles which are persistent colonisers of the exposed pavement.

A short distance to the east of the pavements stands the King Yew (565/002). This veteran tree is 50 feet high and has a girth of over 25 feet. Its age has been estimated at between 400 and 700 years. Another yew of similar age and size can be seen in Hewelsfield churchyard, 1.5 miles to the north (567/022).

The southern part of East Wood is an ancient woodland site, and contains a wide variety of shade-tolerant flowering plants.

Oakhill Wood

Maps 162 and OL14, GR 564/008.   Location sketchmap see page 8. Parking: Lay-by 2.5 miles S of St. Briavels on B4228.

Tracks and paths through FC woodland. Mainly easy walking with some slopes. Going can be very muddy.

As befits its name, this mixed wood has its share of oaks though it cannot boast any of the region's most notable examples. Even so, a bumper acorn harvest and extensive hidden depths ensure its popularity with that most decorative member of the crow family, the jay.

Jays are secretive and suspicious by nature but reveal their presence by the harshness of their screaming call, likened by one eminent naturalist to the tearing of a piece of calico. Although a close approach is difficult, there's no mistaking the jay's colouring, even at a distance for it is our only medium-to-large land bird with prominent blue wing patches. Much of the plumage is pinkish-brown, and this, together with the blue wing flashes and white rump, give a departing jay a distinctly exotic appearance.

The going in parts of Oakhill Wood can be muddy after rain, and stretches of the low-lying path along the northern boundary are covered in liverworts, with ferns and mosses fringing the route.

During July and August, the graceful rose-pink flowers of musk mallow beautify the dry woodland paths and clearings.

From the aptly-named Beech Knoll, at the north-western extremity of the road, there are fine views between the trees beyond Brockweir and over the Wye Valley, reached via the Offa's Dyke Path from Lower Chase at the western tip of the wood.

Clanna Woods ⊕

Maps 162 and OL 14, GR 584/023. Location sketchmap see page 8.
Parking: By FC 'Clanna Woods' notice along 'No Through Road' from u/c crossroads between Hewelsfield and Alvington.

A mixture of good FC rides and rougher grassy paths leading to lake and derelict irrigation canal.

Clanna Woods take their name from a 19th century mansion that stood nearby until its demolition after the Second World War. A scatter of cottages and farm buildings still survive, half-hidden among the trees.

The woodland is of the mixed variety, predominantly beech, sweet chestnut and a blend of conifers, but it is the stretches of water — a lake and the remains of a remarkable miniature canal — that provide the main attractions. To see these, take the wide track dipping through the trees to the right. A quiet approach will not only please the statuesque anglers fly-fishing for trout, but may also enable close-up views to be had of the water birds — coots, moorhens, mallard and little grebes.

The canal to the east and north of the lake, was constructed to supply water to the gardens and glasshouses of the old house. To find it, cross the metal bridge near the weir at the far end of the lake and follow the woodland track to the left. Rapidly going wild now, this enchanting little waterway has an extensive damp-habitat flora and is often frequented by that dainty water-sprite of the bird world, the grey wagtail.

The dried-up beds of smaller ponds can be found nearby and a careful search may reveal a glimpse of the cave which served as an ice-house in the days when Clanna was a rich man's residence.

Bigsweir Wood

Maps 162 and OL 14, GR 545/055. Location sketchmap see page 8 Parking: Along lane signposted 'Offa's Dyke Path' off u/c road from A466, immediately E of Bigsweir Bridge.

Undulating path following Offa's Dyke through 110-acre Woodland Trust woods.

Enter the woodland over a stile and climb to reach and follow the Offa's Dyke long distance path. Glimpses of the Dyke itself, a boundary earthwork dating from Saxon times, can be had along the route.

Bigsweir Wood — or to be more precise Slip Wood, Quicken Tree Wood, Wyeseal Wood and New Weir Grove — comprises the southern portion of a three-mile tract of woodland extending as far north as Lower Redbrook and lining the Gloucestershire bank of the Wye. The Offa's Dyke Path traverses the complete length of this woodland but it is the three-quarter mile section through Bigsweir Wood that we are concerned with here, and which provides woodland walking of exceptional quality.

The soil is acidic in the region and the woodland reflects this. The predominant tree cover is sessile oak and the wood contains many fine veterans, often ivy-clad — a combination guaranteed to attract a good variety of arboreal bird life including several species of tit, nuthatch, great spotted woodpecker and tree creeper. In Spring, the resident bird population is augmented by the arrival of two distinctively-coloured migrants, the redstart and the pied flycatcher, both of which exploit the holes in decaying timber for nest sites.

Ash, beech, holly and yew are also well represented in the Bigsweir woods, as is small-leaved lime, a tree that can easily be overlooked among the burgeoning oaks. Unlike its larger leaved relative, the common lime, the small-leaved is a native British tree, and as pollen analysis of peat has shown, was once much more common than at the present time. The foliage which appears late and is shed early, bears small tufts of reddish hairs, hence the local name, red lime. This tree was once extensively coppiced in these woods, and the stools have frequently grown into fantastic shapes.

Another veteran colonist of acid woodland such as Bigsweir, is the silver birch, which tends to decline as other trees prosper. Consequently, most of the birches along the route are gnarled and decaying specimens bearing a variety of growths. Two which are prominent are the witch's broom, resembling a cluster of sticks and hence often mistaken for a bird's nest or squirrel's drey, and a white bracket fungus popularly known as the razor strop, on account of the use to which it was formerly put by countrymen.

Vast blocks of quartz conglomerate, locally called pudding stone, also occur along the route, their rough outline often softened by cushions of moss and a lush growth of ferns. The commonest

of these are the strap-shaped hartstongue, and the handsome hard fern with the leaflets of its dark green lanceolate leaves widest in the middle. Another distinctive fern, the common polypody, thrives on the stumps of long-felled trees.

It would be hard to imagine a finer wood than this for evoking a feeling of age and continuity, in which man's role, though vital from a conservation standpoint, seems somehow placed into a proper, modest perspective by the giant trees that have towered here for centuries.

Staunton Stones

Maps 162 and OL 14. Parking: Walk 1 — In Staunton village on A4136. Walk 2 — Lay-by on right of A4136, 1 mile W of Staunton

Walk 1 — Short circular walk with rough patches underfoot, and a gradient to reach poised stone and viewpoint.
Walk 2 — Linear walk along FC woodland tracks to rock formation. Steep climb to second of these.

Staunton — 'stony farmstead ' — is aptly named. Within comfortable walking distance of the village can be seen no less than four outstanding natural rock formations, with a man-made standing stone thrown in for good measure.

Searching for these stones, hidden deep in what is to many one of the most appealing corners of the Forest, is an adventure in itself. Legends abound in this area and no wonder, for each stone possesses its own individual character, which no amount of cold, factual geology can dispel.

All the stones lie on FC land and to enable visitors to locate them with the minimum difficulty, the four stones have been arranged in two groups and walking directions provided:

Walk 1 (1 mile):Toad's Mouth Rock (546/127) and Buckstone (542/123)

Walk along the A4136 towards Monmouth. Fifty yards beyond the White Hart Inn, turn left along an unclassified road. The Toad's Mouth Rock is on the right. Legend has it that in prehistoric times, lawbreakers were executed on its flat top.

The Buckstone is reached by following the yellow arrow up the bank on the right just beyond the 15 mph sign. The path climbs over Hymen's Meend (Meend means forest waste). The Buckstone stands near a triangulation pillar. It was a rocking stone until 1885, when a band of irresponsible young men succeeded in toppling it down the slope. It is now pegged and concreted into position. Standing at 900 feet above sea level, the Buckstone is a superb viewpoint from which to survey the Wye Valley and the hills of Wales.

To complete this short walk, turn left to pass the covered reservoir and keep left on a parallel course to that walked earlier, to reach the unclassified road once more. Turn left along it back to the A4136.

Walk 2 (3 miles):Suckstone (542/141) & Near Harkening Rock (543/139) ⊕

Walk towards Staunton. Just before a 'Parking 1 mile' sign, turn left along a woodland track into the Highmeadow Woods. When the track sweeps left, turn right along another track, which in turn soon veers left. The Suckstone is reached in about a mile. It is believed to be the largest single block of stone standing in the country, supposedly weighing between 10,000 and 14,000 tons.

For Near Harkening rock, climb the steep path to the right of the Suckstone, passing several smaller rocks before finally reaching this unusually named stone. Like the Suckstone, Near Harkening Rock is composed of quartz conglomerate (pudding stone). It is said to have got its name from the belief that messages could be transmitted to it through the earth from the rocking Buckstone, a mile or more distant. In more recent times, gamekeepers sheltered beneath its overhang when lying in wait for poachers.

The Long Stone (559/122) can be seen by the A4136, a mile east of Staunton. It stands seven feet high and is believed to have marked the site of a Bronze Age burial place. According to local legend, if it is pricked with a pin at midnight on the summer soltice, the stone will bleed!

Ready Penny & Biblins Car Parks | ⊕

Maps 162 and OL 14. Location sketchmap see page 16. Ready Penny: GR 569/133, Biblins: GR 566/138. Parking: Both sites on B4432, half-a-mile and a mile north of Christchurch respectively.

Two good starting points for exploring the isolated north-west section of the Forest of Dean with steep slopes down wide forest rides to the Wye Valley.

Although not one of the Forest attractions in its own right, Christchurch is notable as being the birthplace of the Forest tourist industry, for in 1938, the first wooden building on the first camp site was officially opened there by Queen Mary.

Ready Penny is a view point with a small car park and picnic place. It also serves as a good starting point for walks through Highmeadow Woods, Mailscot Wood and down to the River Wye at Biblins.

Biblins Car Park is an extensive clearing deep in the woods which, as its name suggests, gives access to Biblins suspension bridge on the River Wye. From there, the old railway along the bank leads north to Symonds Yat East.

The one-and-a-half mile walk down to the Wye entails a stiffish return climb, but the woods are dark, deep and delightful. Ferns flourish in the dappled light, rocky outcrops give a ruggedness to the scene, and the tree-top bird life — tits, nuthatches, woodpeckers — provide interest throughout.

Gaps in the canopy reveal glimpses of buzzards wheeling on high, their plaintive mewing call carrying over the vast expanse of woodland. These handsome predators have made a welcome return to the Forest in recent years and with rabbits in plentiful supply, a reliable food source is readily available.

Towering above its neighbours in a sheltered valley close to the River Wye is Gosling's Ash (553/142). At 108 feet high, this is the tallest broadleaved tree in the Forest, and was named after Sir Arthur Gosling, a local boy who rose through the ranks of the Forestry Commission to become its Director General.

Abundant along the Wye around Biblins suspension bridge is Himalayan balsam, a tall reddish-stemmed plant with pink flowers, the shapes of which have been likened to fairground swingboats. An introduced species, this plant has spread widely along streams and rivers in recent years.

Symonds Yat

**Map 162 and OL 14.
Location sketchmap see page
16.
Yat Rock, GR 563/160
Yat East, GR 561/160
Parking: Yat Rock — In
paying car park on B4432, 3
miles N of Coleford.
Yat East — In 'Pay & Display'
car park near Saracen's Head
Inn.**

*The most popular viewpoint
and riverside walk on the
Wye Valley. Possible
sightings of nesting
peregrines. The swaying
suspension-footbridge
experience is not for
everyone!*

Symonds Yat is a classic example
of a 'honeypot' — a rural attraction suffering from what one
travel writer called 'that gregari-
ous passion which destroys the
object of its love'.

Needless to say, the coach tours
still make for this alluring stretch
of the Wye with its strange-sound-
ing name, where Gloucestershire,
Herefordshire and Gwent (once
Monmouthshire) meet. But it is
the ever-multiplying number of
cars that clog the narrow winding
roads and clutter the parks and
verges that reduce the very name
Symonds Yat to a byword in the
minds of the discerning, on summer weekends at least.

It is of course the view of the
Wye's horseshoe bend from Yat
Rock on which Symonds Yat's
reputation is built, and who can
deny its splendour? And as if that
were not enough, since 1982 visitors in spring have been rewarded
with the additional attraction of a
pair of peregrines, the largest
British members of the falcon
family. Thanks to a vigorous protection campaign carried out by
the RSPB in co-operation with
the FC these have managed to
breed successfully while at the
same time providing visitors with
superb views of their mastery of
the air.

A glance at the map reveals that
Symonds Yat itself is divided into
East and West and a choice of
riverside walks can be taken. A
popular four-mile walk starts at
the 'pay and display' car park
near the Saracen's Head Inn
(561/160) in East Yat, and follows the old railway, now the
Wye Valley Walk, for a mile and a
half downstream to Biblins. Here
the route crosses the suspension
footbridge built by the FC in
1957, before returning on the opposite bank as far as Yat West,
from where a ferry at Ye Olde
Ferrie Inne crosses the Wye back
to the start.

The Forest of Dean

Because of its geographical isolation, the Forest of Dean has always been considered as a region with its own distinctive character. This is to a large extent still true, for the Forest proper — 27,000 acres, of which 22,000 acres are under plantation — is Crown land, adminstered by the Forestry Commission.

Fortunately for those wishing to explore the Forest on foot, access to these Forestry Commission woodlands presents no problems. In the words of one of the Commission's own recent guidebooks: 'The Forest system of rides and tracks is always open to walkers, except where forestry operations are taking place, and warning notices are displayed'. This freedom to roam, long taken for granted in the Forest, remains a pipe-dream elsewhere, both in Gloucestershire and further afield. However, exercising this freedom is not quite as easy as it at first sounds. Rides and tracks are so numerous and landmarks so few and far between that trouble-free Forest walking requires both a working knowledge of the geography of the region and some awareness of the subtle differences in terrain and scenery. What at first sight may appear as trees, trees and more trees is in fact a region of considerable diversity.

In recent years, the Forestry Commission has produced a number of excellent, inexpensive leaflets on waymarked walks starting from car parks and picnic places scattered across the Forest. Details of these can be obtained from the Commission at Crown Office, Bank Street, Coleford, Glos. (Telephone 0594 33057).

Rather than duplicate the instructions given in these leaflets, this section of the book attempts to provide useful background information on the region, as well as assisting and advising readers who prefer to plan their own visits to this largely unexplored part of the county.

Any consideration of the Forest of Dean inevitably raises the question of its age. That there were extensive areas of wildwood here in prehistoric times, there can be no doubt. However, the evolution of its earliest human inhabitants from hunter-gatherers to farmers resulted in forest-clearance beginning in the New Stone Age. This process accelerated with the discovery, first of iron, and later of coal, evidence of the early mining of which can still be seen today.

Despite these inroads into the ancient wildwood, the Forest must have retained much more of its primeval state than neighbouring areas for it was established as a royal hunting forest by decree of King Canute in 1016. The Normans in their turn maintained the Dean's special status. King William the Conqueror hunted here in 1069, and it is recorded that King John's favourite dish was Dean wild boar. The laws protecting the royal game were strict and rigorously applied. A Forest constable was appointed, supervising the domain from his castle at St. Briavels, for in those times the Forest extended in a vast triangle from the Wye to the Severn and northwards to the Leadon.

But the King's hunting ground in Gloucestershire was more than mere woodland. Some idea of its diversity can be gained from its description in Marwood's 'Lawes of the Forest (1598)':-

'A certain territorie of woody ground and fruitful pastures, priviledged for wild beasts and foules of forest, chase and warren to rest and abide there, in the save protection of the King, for his princely delight and pleasure.'

Despite its unique status as a royal playground, the tree-felling that had been steadily increasing in the Dean since the Middle Ages, continued into Tudor times, not only to build warships, but also to fuel the charcoal-hungry iron forges. The ships and weapons derived from Dean oaks were held in such dread by the Spanish, that officers leading the Armada were given specific instructions to fell the Forest trees as soon as they had made good their invasion.

What the Spanish failed to do, was accomplished less than a century later by a grasping Englishman. In 1640, Sir John Wyntour purchased over 18,000 acres of the Forest from Charles I and proceeded to fell 20,000 of the best trees. It took the expanding needs of the Royal Navy, culminating in the personal involvement of Lord Nelson, to see a long overdue attempt made to make good these depredations, and it is the surviving plantings from the Napoleonic war period that are the veteran broadleaved trees of today's Forest.

The twentieth century brought mixed fortunes for the Forest. Although the age of wooden warships had passed, the timber needs of two world wars saw felling on a drastic scale in Crown woodlands. The creation of the Forestry Commission in 1924 heralded much replanting, involving the widespread introduction of conifers, but since the designating of Dean as the country's first Forest Park in 1938, the planting of oak and beech have at last begun the lengthy process of restoring the Dean to something like its former glory.

Industry meanwhile, has declined throughout the Forest. The ironworks and deep coal mines have closed, as have all but one of the stoneworks. The railways, too, have disappeared, apart from a single tourist enterprise at Norchard, near Lydney. A handful of small and privately-owned drift mines still linger on here among the trees and bracken, but the scars of quarrying and mining are fast being obliterated.

Of the exercising of commoners' rights, another once-distinctive feature of Forest life, only the sheep and a few pigs remain. Until 1975, horses, cattle and poultry roamed freely but new bye-laws banished them, to join the wild boar in the history books.

So what, apart from its trees, does the Forest offer today? The towns — Coleford, Cinderford and Lydney — are, to say the least, uninspiring. The villages — bearing in mind that it was not until the last century that they were allowed within the Forest bounds — are, with the exception of St. Briavels, Staunton, Newland and a handful of others, equally unremarkable.

That leaves the tourist havens — Dean Heritage Centre at Soudley, Clearwell Caves, Puzzle Wood, Littledean Hall — each well worth a visit, each contributing something to an undertanding of the shaping of the present Forest.

But it is by taking full advantage of the freedom to roam and, at the same time, giving full reign to our curiosity and sense of romance for the past, that we can best experience the rare magic of the Forest. For despite all the changes that have taken place here over the centuries, a great deal of that indefinable magic remains.

A winterclad Freeminer of a century ago

Merring Meend Heath & Viewpoint ⊕

Maps 162 and OL 14, GR 658/169.
Parking: In FC car park on east of A4136, one-and-a-half miles S Mitcheldean.

Two constrasting attractions — an open grassy viewpoint and a biologically-interesting wetland area, lying on either side of the A4136.

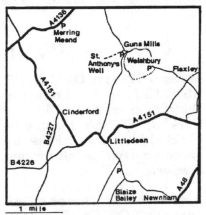

Standing 800ft. above sea-level, Merring Meend is a rugged hilltop bisected by the A4136, and commanding impressive views both eastwards to the Severn and south and west over the Forest.

Though limited in extent, it offers plenty of interest. Those wishing to climb for the best views should leave the car park and walk up past the old quarry. Here. despite some obstruction from tall conifers, the aspect makes the effort well worthwhile. Above the car park, an expanse of short-cropped turf scattered with oaks, is ideal for play, picnicking and family exploration generally, with the fringe vegetation of gorse, brambles and bracken adding a touch of the wild to the setting.

The word meend, signifying waste or open ground, occurs fairly widely in the Forest and the small portion of Merring Meend on the western side of the A4136 is a remnant of the heathland that once formed a considerable part of the Dean.

This area of a mere four acres is managed by the GTNC who endeavour to prevent gorse and bracken from overgrowing the heather and cross-leaved heath that comprise the natural ground cover on the drier land.

Close by can be seen three small fragments of natural wetland — a pond and two patches of acid bog — which are even more valuable survivals of the ancient Forest. Here is one of the few remaining Gloucestershire localities of the bog bean, or buckbean, a distinctive water plant with large trifoliate leaves and spikes of pink and white, five-petalled flowers. These are at their best in May and June, and are followed by a range of

23

other wetland flowering plants, including marsh violet, water mint and bulrush.

The pond is well stocked with fish by a local angling club but, more importantly, provides a valuable breeding site for smooth and palmate newts. Sedge warblers pour forth their chattering song throughout the spring and early summer.

Welshbury Fort

Maps 162 and OL 14, GR 683/157. Location sketchmap see page 23. Parking: Off u/c Flaxley — Mitcheldean road. Park by second barrier on left beyond Flaxley.

Ancient earthwork on remote FC-owned hilltop with access via clearly defined woodland paths.

Welshbury is a vast rectangular entrenchment, almost centainly an Iron Age hill fort, crowning the summit of Welshbury Wood. It was defended by a single bank and ditch on the north and east sides, and by a triple rampart on the south and west. The single entrance is at the south-east corner.

To reach it, go through the barrier and climb steadily, noting on the right a seat erected in memory of a local forester. Those with plenty of time and/or an adventurous disposition will want to find their own way to the top, but the steady plodders and those who prefer to know exactly what lies ahead, should follow the wide forest ride, eventually crossing the stile leading up to the fort entrance.

In spring, the way is gladdened, as in so many Forest woods, by drift upon drift of bluebells. Later, they are succeeded by a predictable variety of other shade-tolerant plants, while a late summer visit offers luscious blackberries as a tasty bonus.

The fort itself is a stone and branch-strewn expanse topped by some truly splendid old beeches, the surface roots of which writhe over the sparsely-clad ground. From April to July, the songs of chiffchaffs and willow warblers rise above the distant din of human activity below, while in places, fleeting glimpses can be had through the tree crowns of faraway slopes and scattered habitations.

Welshbury is just about as far removed from the run-of-the-mill tourist attraction as you could wish to find — and all the better for that.

St. Anthony's Well

Maps 162 and OL 14, GR 669/158. Location sketchmap see page 23.
Parking: On verge near junction of u/c Flaxley — Mitcheldean and Flaxley — Littledean roads at Guns Mills (676/159).
Access: About half-a-mile's walk along unmetalled track at side of old mill.

Fresh water spring in woodland glade, hidden deep in the Forest.

Not far distant from Welshbury's lone hilltop, at the end of a woodland track alongside a tiny valley, is St. Anthony's Well. A stone-lined hollow fed by a spring, it lies half-hidden by luxuriant ferns beneath the dappled shade of ancient beeches. Beyond, a bluebell wood stretches away up the slopes, while all round can be seen giant mossy boulders of pudding stone.

A secret, romantic forest corner indeed! But there is more to this quiet hollow than its beauty, for the cool waters that surface here have for centuries been credited with amazing healing powers. Before the Dissolution, monks from nearby Flaxley Abbey sent sufferers with skin ailments to bathe in the well on the first nine mornings in May. Later, the waters were reputed to possess the power to heal mangy dogs, which had to be thrown into the water three times at sunrise.

Even to the present day, faith in the health-giving water from St.Anthony's Well remains undiminished, at least with the old folk. It is said to be a sure cure for all manner of eye disorders — and that's not just eyewash!

The oddly appealing group of buildings known as Guns Mills is a survivor of long-lost industrial endeavour. As far back as the early 17th century, blast furnaces worked here, producing guns for the Crown for use in Holland and later in the Civil War. Paper-making followed. Those with a liking for industrial archaeology will enjoy exploring the crumbling ruins along the streamside on the way up to the well.

Blaize Bailey $\quad | \oplus$

Maps 162 and OL 14, GR 662/117. Location sketchmap see page 23. Parking: Signposted car park off u/c Littledean — Soudley road.

Forest-fringe viewpoint. Walking opportunities to suit most tastes. Ideal for families. Toilets.

Blaize Bailey is a superb viewpoint on the eastern ridge of the Forest, looking out over the Severn's dramatic loop around the Arlingham peninsula. The historic town of Newnham (see page 41) linked by footpath via Pleasant Stile, lies little more than a mile distant, as does sprawling Cinder-ford to the north, but Blaize Bailey still retains its lofty splendour, isolated from such meaner levels of existence, in its wooded fastness.

Close by, alongside the tree-fringed road from Littledean, and linked to it by a footpath, lie four of the five Soudley Ponds, created in the 1850s as fish ponds. One of the quartet is still stocked for the use of anglers, but all are now designated as part of a Site of Special Scientific Interest. It is easy to understand why, for dragonflies and damselflies abound in the summer sunshine, and water-loving plants ensure a changing pageant of colour from spring onwards.

Wench Ford & Blackpool Bridge $\quad | \oplus$

Maps 162 and OL 14, GR 654/081. Location sketchmap see page 27. Parking: Along forest road, off B4431, 3 miles E of Parkend.

Popular streamside picnic and barbeque site with toilets. Forest walking and nearby historic features.

Just south of Blackpool Bridge, a stretch of old railway line parallel to the B4431 has been desig-nated as a picnic site and offers ample parking, plus barbeques — with facilities for portable BBQs too. So if your idea of happiness is eating out alfresco-style beneath the oaks by the banks of a meandering forest stream, here's the very place.

Like so many Forest locations however, visited in mid-week or out of season, this is a delightful spot. At these times, the bands of scavenging chaffinches, having reverted to their natural mode of life in the absence of visitors, soon reappear hopefully, leaving the tits and treecreepers to forage alone in the trees.

The Blackpool Brook is a joy, both for paddling and for the opportunities it provides for watching wild life or just relaxing. Above, by the forest fringe, mossy mats of tree roots overhang the embankment of the long-gone railway. Nearby, rampant foxgloves splash gaudy colour by the edge of a tumbling tributary rushing to meet the larger stream.

The section of old road exposed by the brook near Blackpool

Bridge was once believed to be of Roman origin. This theory has since been discounted, but there is no question that the road is of ancient origin.

By the woodland edge, a short distance to the north, to the right of the road to Upper Soudley, can be seen the Drummer Boy Stone. This is a hollowed-out block of quartz congomerate (pudding stone) containing traces of smelted iron. Its age and the origin of its name are uncertain, but it is without doubt an unusual relic of early industry in this part of the Forest.

Mallards Pike ⊕

Maps 162 and OL 14, GR 638/090.
Parking: FC car park off B4431, 2 miles E Parkend.

Popular recreational location with two small lakes and easy walking. Ideal for families with pushchairs. Disabled access. Toilets.

Two secret lakes hidden in the heart of the forest — what bliss! Yet if you search for Mallards Pike on a map published prior to 1982, you will search in vain for the lakes have only been recently created by the damming of a forest stream. If you visit Mallards

Pike off-season, a good deal of the magic still clings but, at other times, the mallards themselves are crowded out by canoes, sailing dinghies — and civilisation.

So time your visit carefully, park, picnic if you wish, and savour the sunshine filtering through the conifers. The walks are easy — both to find and to follow — and apart from the predictable conifers, variety is added by plantings of beech, oak, birch, yew and holly.

Bird life is plentiful whatever the time of year, especially tits and tiny industrious goldcrests, while tufted ducks — the drakes looking strikingly handsome in their black and white plumage — grace the placid surface of the lake.

Those wishing to wander into the woods have a choice of attractions, of which New Fancy (west) and Blackpool Bridge (east) are both close at hand.

New Fancy View & Forest Walk ⊕

Maps 162 and OL 14, GR 627/095.   Location sketchmap see page 27. Parking: Car park off u/c road linking B4226 at Speech House and B4431.

Old   colliery   site transformed into tourist attraction.   Popular viewpoint and leisure area with easy Forest access. Toilets.

For over a century, until 1944, waste from the New Fancy colliery was tipped here, creating a spoil heap estimated at three-quarters of a million tons. In the 1960s, two-thirds of this vast mound was taken away to be used as part of the foundations for a new steel works in South Wales. What remained was landscaped, grassed and planted with trees — and New Fancy was born again, this time as a tourist attraction.

The energetic will want to climb the well-trodden path up to the viewpoint, the reward being a sweeping panorama over the eastern expanse of the Forest. Close by stands the 'Two Million Acre Stone', unveiled by the Chairman of the Forestry Commission in 1976 to commemorate the Commission's achievement in planting two million acres of woodland in Britain between the years 1919 and 1976.

An easy two-and-a-half mile circular walk can be taken from the car park along two lengths of old railway line and back past the site of the gravitation shunting sidings of the old colliery. Lumps of coal can still be picked up around here as evidence of a mine that produced over three-and-a-half million tons of 'black diamonds' during its 113-year working life, a period that spanned the boom years of the Forest of Dean coal industry.

Nagshead

**Maps 162 and OL 14, GR 605/084.   Location sketchmap see page 27.
Parking: RSPB car park, off B4331, on W edge of Parkend.**

A 750-acre RSPB/FC managed oakwood bird reserve with public access. Plenty of woodland paths and marked trails.

To Gloucestershire birdwatchers, Nagshead is associated instantly with the pied flycatcher. As long ago as 1942, in an attempt to increase the population of tit species to help control leaf-eating caterpillars, nestboxes were introduced in Nagshead Plantation. To the surprise of the ornithologists involved, fifteen of the eighty-four boxes were occupied by pied flycatchers, attractive relatives of the common spotted flycatcher and a bird about which comparatively little was known.

Since then, both this little bird, and another colourful summer visitor, the redstart, have regularly used the nestboxes, together with several species of the tit family for which the artificial nest-site scheme was originally intended.

In recent years, over 300 of the numbered boxes have been used altogether, and children in particular will enjoy spotting them as they follow the paths through the reserve.

Although small, the pied flycatcher can be easily identified by the patient observer. Like its spotted relative, it has an upright stance when perched, and frequently sallies forth to capture small insects. However, it differs from the spotted flycatcher in that it seldom returns to the same perch and often alights on the ground. The handsome male bird is black above and pure white below, while the less conspicuous female has olive-brown upper parts. Both sexes display prominent white wing areas in flight.

Apart from its bird population, Nagshead is one of the finest areas of mature oak wood in the Forest. A rich acidic flora flourishes on the well-drained soils. Visitors in July and early August stand a good chance of seeing the striking white admiral butterfly, gatherings of which sometimes feed on bramble blossom in the woodland clearings.

Cannop Valley

⊕

Maps 162 and OL 14, GR 610/107. Location sketchmap see page 27. Parking: Car park off B4226 on Speech House side of B4226/B4234 junction.

Picnic site near large ponds in delightful wooded setting. Varied choice of walks.

Paradoxically, it was the Industrial Revolution that created the two large ponds that draw anglers, birdwatchers and other seekers after the quiet life to the Cannop Valley.

For until the early years of the 19th century, the tiny Cannop Brook flowed unnoticed through the Forest glades half-a-mile south-west from Speech House. Then, one-and-a-half miles to the south, new ironworks were built at Parkend and it was decided to drive the blast furnaces and steam hammers by means of a giant wheel, powered by water provided by the Cannop Brook. This meant damming the brook and creating two artificial ponds, which fulfilled their intended function until the closure of the ironworks in the early years of the present century.

Since then, Cannop Ponds have become one of the Forest's 'natural' attractions — well stocked with fish and populated with mallard, coot and moorhen. The banks in their tree-fringed setting are ideal for gentle strolls, waterside picnics and quiet contemplation — weekends and bank holidays excepted.

By the southern extremity of the lower pond can be seen — and heard — the last surviving stone works in the Forest. Until earlier in the century, locally-quarried stone arrived here by tramway. Now, however, the grey and blue Pennant sandstone is transported in 5- to 10-ton blocks by lorry, and is sawn into suitable size for use in ornamental masonry.

In the woods to the west can be seen the Bixslade quarries, silent now, but once some of the most productive and profitable in the entire Forest.

Between the upper pond and the B4226, lies Cannop Bridge Marsh, an area of marsh and mixed woodland, now a GTNC reserve. There is a good wetland plant population and the alder carr provides suitable habitat for reed bunting, marsh tit, chiffchaff and wood warbler.

Speech House

⊕

Maps 162 and OL 14, GR 620/121. Location sketchmap see page 27. Parking: Speech House car park off B4226 between Cinderford and Coleford.

Good centre for miles of walking along both forest tracks and paths. Sculpture trail. Picnic areas with toilets.

The traditional centre of the Forest of Dean, Speech House is perhaps the most familiar name in the whole of the region. Standing on the B4226 between Cinderford and Coleford, it was built in 1680 as a hunting lodge for Charles II. Later, it became the meeting place of the Forest verderers and is now a hotel. Within easy walking distance of Speech House are several interesting features.

On either side of the B4226 stand two fine oaks. **The Sanzen-Baker Oak** (617/119) is named after the Forest's Deputy Surveyor (1954-1968), who is remembered as the man who encouraged the public to explore the Forest. Planted in 1810, this oak is 80 feet high and has a girth of ten feet.

The Verderers' Oak (619/119) is only 55 feet high, but its 23-foot girth qualifies it as the Forest's stoutest oak. Approximately 300 to 400 years old, this tree commemorates the verderers, who maintained the Forest from the days of King Canute. Its small crown indicates that at some stage it lost some of its upper branches to illegal lopping, possibly by coppice-cutters.

Nearby are the **King Edward VII Yews** (619/122). This group of distinctive evergreens was planted in 1902 to mark the King's coronation. East of Speech House in the **Arboretum** (623/122). This is a mixed collection of over 200 varieties of conifers and broadleaved trees and shrubs, the planting of which began in 1916. Of special interest is the dawn redwood, a deciduous conifer thought to be extinct until its was found growing in China in the 1940s.

Speech House Lake (626/114) was formed in 1974 by the damming of the Blackpool Brook. It serves as a nature reserve and its fringes support the colourful wild iris as well as a good dragonfly population.

Starting from the car park is the four-mile **Forest Sculpture Trail**, featuring sculptures in a variety of materials arranged in a woodland setting, guaranteed to provide a Forest walk with a difference.

Woorgreens Lake & Marsh

Map 162 and OL 14, GR 630/126. Location sketchmap see page 27.
Parking: Off B4226 between Speech House and Dilke Hospital.

Expanse of wetland habitat of special natural history interest, managed by GTNC.

It was not until 1981 that open-cast coal mining ceased in this area of the Forest of Dean. Yet since that time, the reclamation of the resulting wasteland in the interest of aquatic wild life has been so successful that the site is not only the best for dragonflies in the entire Forest, but is also regarded as of national importance. This success is attributed to a rapid colonisation both by plants and insects and the careful control of water levels by means of a sluice.

From the B4226, roughly midway between Speech House and Dilke Hospital, cross the stile in the fence and see for yourself just how quickly and effectively nature with man's help will heal a ravaged landscape.

Choose a fine day in June and you stand a fair chance of spotting several of the seventeen dragonfly species recorded here over the past decade. These include the four-spotted chaser, the southern hawker and the emperor, as well as several species of rare damselflies.

Bird watchers, too, will find Worgreens rewarding. Mallard, teal and tufted duck breed around the island, waders such as the curlew and green sandpiper, are occasional visitors, and snipe find the winter conditions favourable. Routine conservation management work is essential to maintain a nature reserve such as this in its optimum state. This is carried out by the GTNC and involves the control of willow and bulrush, and the clearing of ditches.

Over Severn

The least-known part of Gloucestershire, Over Severn, is the area which lies in the north-west corner of the county bordered by the hilly north-eastern rim of the Forest of Dean and the River Severn between Gloucester and Tewkesbury.

To the north lies the Ledbury area of Herefordshire (now officially Hereford and Worcester), with the M50 motorway sweeping through this once quiet pastoral borderland. The Over Severn region is drained by the little River Leadon, which rises in the gentle hills near Ledbury and flows over rich red soils in a south-easterly direction to contribute its waters to the Severn near Over Bridge, close by Gloucester.

Over Severn boasts only one town, Newent, and one prominent landmark, May Hill, but it has its share of lesser riches too, even if they need to be searched for. Perhaps the most endearing of these are the wild daffodils, which spread like a creamy-yellow tide along the lanes and over the fields, woods and orchards in spring.

In addition, the region is blessed with some delightful woodland, which it shares with its Herefordshire neighbour. It also contains a cluster of pleasant, often elusive villages, of which Dymock, famed for its association-swith a group of distinguished poets earlier this century, is the most notable.

Dymock Woods

Maps 149 and 162.
GRs: Queen's Wood, 677/285,
Hay Wood, 685/273,
Dymock Wood, 692/285.
Parking: Queen's Wood, FC car park, off u/c Newent—Kempley road.
Hay Wood, also off u/c Newent—Kempley road, along lane signposted 'Linton and Gorsley'. Dymock Wood, along lane signposted 'Norman's Land and Dymock' from Four Oaks.

About four square miles of FC woodland, crossed by graded shale rides providing all-weather walking, as well as plenty of secondary paths.

Dymock Woods — comprising Queen's Wood, Hay Wood and Dymock Wood — straddle the Gloucestershire-Herefordshire border to the west of the Newent—Dymock road.

Until the M50 motorway carved a great swathe through their very heart, these woods lay in the untroubled depths of a gentle landscape of tiny hamlets and farms scattered amid lush pastures, a land of wild daffodils immortalised by poets, yet virtually unknown to all but the most discerning of travellers.

1 mile

But the coming of the motorway age changed all that. The planners' decision to construct the so-called Ross spur westwards from the M5, brought the hideous din of our own troubled times into this rural backwater and the precious peace of Dymock Woods has gone for ever.

And yet, despite what has been done in the name of progress, to the woods, there is indeed life after the motorway! There may be no escaping the incessant rush and rumble, but those twin healers, time and nature, working as ever in complete harmony, have somehow managed to soften the harsh impact of this intrusion and restore something of the beauty of the Dymock Woods, each of which has its own individual character and is worthy of consideration in its own right.

Queen's Wood largest and best-known of the trio, offers a spacious car park, picnic benches and an open expanse of cut grass — ideal in other words for a family afternoon out.

Once away from the car park, however, the conifers close in. Cones litter the paths and by collecting and examining them, together with the trees themselves, it is possible to identify the main softwood trees — the evergreen Douglas fir and Norway spruce and the deciduous larches (European, Japanese and hybrid species) are all grown here.

This is not to say that hardwood trees have no place in Queen's Wood. A careful examination reveals beech to be the dominant broadleaved type, with birch, oak and rowan in support. On the woodland floor, the primroses and wild daffodils of spring are succeeded by dainty wood sorrel, which in turn gives way to bold stands of foxglove and rosebay willowherb.

Search deep in the wood and you will come upon a delightful little lake, complete with its own island, on which mallard and moorhen can nest undisturbed, seemingly oblivious of the constant swish of motorway traffic beyond the beech glades.

Hay Wood, bisected by the un-classified road linking the B4221 at Gorsley with the B4215 south of Dymock, is the smallest of the Dymock Woods. There are sev-

eral parking opportunities along the little-used road, although those who prefer to keep to well-established paths should use the one given above which has a picnic bench, and from which a woodland track, marked by red posts, can be followed.

As in Queen's Wood, conifers are predominant, but little spinneys of broadleaved trees, chiefly oaks, ensure that a varied walk can be taken to the southern extremities of the wood, from where the jarring drone of the motorway fades into oblivion.

Dymock Wood is the most northerly, and therefore the closest to Dymock, of the woods grouped under the name of this Gloucestershire village. It lies astride the Daffodil Way, an eight-mile circular route established in 1988. This footpath enables walkers to enjoy an absorbing way-marked ramble through countryside over which public rights of way had been for years little used and consequently poorly maintained. As its name suggests, this walk extends through the heart of the'Daffodil Country', and Dymock Wood is one the strongholds of this declining wild relative of the ubiquitous cultivated daffodil, from which it is easily distinguished by its smaller, paler flowers.

Long-lived locals can recall when these daffodils were picked by what the Ledbury-born poet, John Masefield, described as 'Hard-featured women, weatherbeaten brown' - for sale in Birmingham and other distant cities. The daffodils may have dwindled in number, but at least they have survived, which is more than can be said for the railway along which the 'Daffodil specials' once ran.

The wild daffodils may be Dymock Wood's main attraction but the advancing year brings other delights to replace them. Of particular beauty is the elegant and aptly-named pendulous sedge, while wild cherry, broom and honeysuckle splash their distinctive colour, and bilberry fruit can be sought in the dry areas of the wood.

A word of warning to would-be picnickers. On no account settle down in the vicinity of a wood ants' nest. They are fascinating to watch — one colony favoured pine needles, another preferred the sheaths of beech buds — but their bite is exceedingly painful!

May Hill

**Map 162, GR 696/213.
Parking: On u/c road at GR 691/211, Yartleton Lane, from A40, three-quarters of a mile W of Huntley. Footpath to hill on right.**

Isolated NT-owned hill, with superb views and bracing walking.

Rising to 971 feet above sea level, the symmetrical cone of May Hill is one of Gloucestershire's best known, yet least visited landmarks. Overlooking the Forest of Dean, yet apart from it, this fine isolated hill is close in geological affinity to the Malverns, sharing as it does the Llandovery sandstones of the Silurian period with the western flanks of the famous Worcestershire range. May Hill has its limestone bed too — the so-called Woolhope limestone — and such a mixture of rocks has in its turn produced varying soils with a diverse flora.

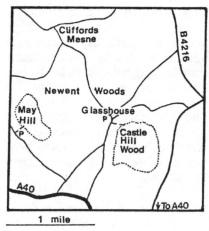

No trees in Gloucestershire are gazed at from afar more than the tall Scots pines of May Hill. These giants were planted in 1887 to commemorate Queen Victoria's Golden Jubilee, and have taken the place of earlier trees that once crowned this windswept hilltop. In their turn too, the present pines will give way to successors, which are already growing nearby.

Earlier this century, John Mase-

36

field, born not far away at Ledbury, and destined to be Poet Laureate, captured in verse the sight of a solitary ploughman on May Hill:

*'Ploughing the hill with steady
yoke*
*Of pine trees lightning-struck and
broke.*
*I've marked the May Hill plough-
man stay*
There on his hill, day after day,
Driving his team against the sky.'

The ploughman may have finally plodded homeward long ago, but May Hill's skyscape is as striking as ever. And what views! The eye can wander freely in every direction, taking in the Malverns, the Forest of Dean, the Vale of Severn and the scarp of the Cotswolds. While away on the far horizon rise the dramatic Brecon Beacons and a ring of other peaks fading into vast ethereal distance.

Yartleton was once the name by which this hill was known and it is appropriate that the approach road and a nearby farm both perpetuate this ancient word, derived from the Celtic for round-topped hill. The change of name to May Hill came about through two customs, both taking place on May Day. One of these related to com-moners' rights, to which nearby parishes were entitled. By tradition, representatives of these parishes met on the hill on May Day morning to resolve any matters concerning the common.

The other custom was much more colourful and possibly of older origin. Groups of young people from local villages gathered on the hilltop to enact the symbolic battle between winter and summer, which resulted in the inevitable overthrow of winter. The event concluded with the victorious 'summer' party returning home bearing budding branches and spring flowers as tokens of their season's triumph.

Keen walkers may wish to explore two contrasting areas adjacent to May Hill. One is the tract of common land to the north, in the direction of Cliffords Mesne. A clear path can be followed through the scrub and bracken, down to reach the continuation of Yartleton Lane. Descending past the Yew Tree Inn, turn right into the lane to Glasshouse, which can be followed through Newent Woods. In two miles, just before reaching Glasshouse, a stile on the right gives access to a footpath, which climbs through the woods back to May Hill.

Castle Hill Wood, Glasshouse

Map 162, GR 712/210.
Location sketchmap see page 36.
Parking: Roadside verge, Glasshouse, 2 miles NW junction of A40 and B4216.

Private woodland with network of public footpaths. Wet patches, steep gradients and late-summer bramble encroachment.

Glasshouse is a hamlet near the eastern foot of May Hill and as the inn sign shows, was once known for its glass-blowing industry. Today, its topiary is the chief attraction, apart from the snug little inn itself. Behind the inn lies Castle Hill Wood which, despite being privately owned, is criss-crossed by footpaths, several of which skirt the earthwork hidden among the trees near its highest and northern extremity.

So, if your idea of an afternoon's outing with a difference, is a game of 'hunt the earthwork', Castle Hill Wood could well be what you are looking for. All you have to do is to follow the drive signposted 'No bridleway. Thank you' a few yards up the hill from the inn. A short walk brings you to the wood, and soon the search is on. Don't expect to find the remains of a castle, despite the name of the wood. The likelihood is that the fortification you are seeking was little more than a look-out post, built by the Iron Age inhabitants of the area, say about 500 BC. The object of your quest is a small square earthwork, surrounded by a ditch, and dominated by a venerable old yew tree, flanked by two impressive veteran oaks. Locating this 'castle' not only gives a sense of achievement; there is something strangely fulfilling in gazing upon a remnant of our prehistoric past — albeit a somewhat unremarkable one — that few others have heard of, let alone seen.

Finally, a word of advice. The paths in Castle Hill Wood can be very muddy after rain, so strong footwear is essential. Also the brambles that encroach from late summer onwards are of a particularly vicious and resilient variety, so wear resistant clothing and carry a stout stick if you tackle the climb at that time of year.

Severn Vale

From Twyning, north of Tewkesbury, southwards as far as the M4 road bridge at Beachley — a distance of almost 50 miles — the Severn is a Gloucestershire river. During that journey, Britain's longest river changes from a swiftly purposeful middle stage to a mile-wide tidal estuary, with its tortuous meandering course between Minsterworth and Frampton between the two. This latter is the stretch of river famous for its bore, a tidal wave which surges upstream amd which, during the spring and autumn equinoxes, can attain a height of up to ten feet.

The strip of country along the banks of the Severn, sandwiched as it were between the Forest of Dean and the Cotswolds, is known as the Severn Vale — a low-lying pastoral countryside, shaped and still profoundly influenced by the proximity of the great river. This is a region with age-old traditions of fishing for eels, elvers and salmon, a landscape through which river — and later — canal craft have long sailed for trade and pleasure, and over which vast flocks of waders and waterfowl are a commonplace sight.

It follows that river views — and riverside walking — both feature in the sites chosen to represent this section. There is variety too, provided among others by a deer park, an exceptional village green, two canals, woodland, and two Cotswold outlier hills left stranded by the march of geological time.

Finally, progressing northwards, is ancient, historic Tewkesbury, commanding the confluence of the Avon and Severn, and providing a unique contribution to the character of the Severn Vale.

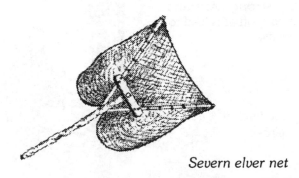

Severn elver net

Upper Common, Aylburton ⊕

Map 162 and OL 14, GR 608/022.
Parking: On edge of common, along lefthand fork at top of Chapel Hill, Aylburton.

Small bracken-clad common overlooking River Severn from where a few grassy tracks and footpaths lead to nearby woodland.

Upper Common is a bracken-clad expanse above Aylburton village, dotted with a scattering of oak, birch and Scots pine. Children will love to play hide-and-seek here, or take turns on the solitary swing. Grown-ups meanwhile, cannot fail to admire the sweeping views of the Severn, and especially of its suspension bridge. Alternatively, in late summer, family blackberry-picking may well prove popular.

Though close to the Severn, the pull of the Forest is equally strong here and tempting footpaths lead to the woods.

Workaday Aylburton is notable for two reasons. Its parish church, which stood formerly high on Chapel Hill, was dismantled in the 1850s and rebuilt in the village. Its 14th century preaching cross, battered but mercifully spared the fussy 'improvements' rendered to so many others, was also moved, from the centre of the road to its present place at the foot of Chapel Hill.

Aylburton Cross

40

Newnham-on-Severn

Map 162.
River Frontage:GR 695/120
Parking: Riverside car park.
Newnham   Green: GR 689/115.
Parking: Alongside green.

Small, historic town with two pleasant open spaces, suitable for family exploration. Toilets by River Frontage.

Like William Wordsworth, Newnham-on-Severn is most often associated with daffodils but is worthy of wider recognition. Many visitors admire only its lofty church perched high on sandstone cliffs, and the nodding flowers as they climb or descend the main street. A pity, for Newnham still has plenty of reminders of the prosperity it knew before the cutting of the Sharpness — Gloucester canal robbed it of its trade and influence and reduced it to the pretty-country-town image it has had to settle for since.

While a good deal of present-day Newnham can be seen on a town walkabout, it is from the two traffic-free open spaces referred to above that we can best appreciate its former significance.

River Frontage
A small inviting area of grassland extends from the car park at the foot of the hill on the northern edge of the town. Wander along the shore line here, watching the river ebb and flow. Or sit on a seat under the birches and take in at leisure the scenic sweep embracing Westbury church spire, Garden Cliff, and the distant Cotswold escarpment. Closer at hand, beyond the reeds and stands of sea-aster, herons stalk at low tide and gulls and waders exploit the Severn's bounty.

It was the river's caprice that made Newnham, only to reduce it later to backwater status. Almost half a mile wide at high tide, the Severn in 1171 carried Richard le Clare, Earl of Pembroke — the original Strongbow — from Newnham with his army to conquer Ireland, bearing weapons made from Forest of Dean iron. Later, the town, one of the five Great Boroughs of Gloucester, re-

41

ceived kings almost as a matter of course. Henry II, John —who presented Newnham with a sword — Edward II and Edward III, all visited what was then Gloucestershire's most important town west of the Severn.

The kings have long gone, of course, but majesty of a different kind comes to Newnham still, in the form of the Severn bore, a powerful tidal wave that sweeps up the river and can reach heights of up to 10 feet as it passes the town twice daily on about 130 days each year with the high spring tides.

Newnham Green
This delightful open space in two parts lies opposite the church at the top of the hill. That nearest the church was the site of the town's castle, which is said to have been garrisoned by Royalist troops during the Civil War but which has since disappeared apart from vestiges of the ramparts seen here. The view of the river downstream is superb, and the little sheltered dell dominated by a single wellingtonia tree, is ideal for children's games.

The second part of the green is reached over a footbridge and comprises a wooded ridge with the old pound (an enclosure for stray livestock) at its far extremity. Sweeping views over a panorama of infinite variety makes this one of the best vantage points in the Severn Vale.

Garden Cliff, Strand, Westbury-on-Severn

Map 162, GR 716/133.
Location sketchmap see page 41.
Parking: In Westbury village on A48 between Gloucester and Lydney.
Access to cliff: Along footpath on right down lane beyond church to track by restored mill. Turn left for foot of cliff.

A low-tide, beachcombing wander along the Severn foreshore.
Wellies essential.

Mention the word garden in connection with Westbury-on-Severn and most people will conjure up an impression of the delightful National Trust water garden on the edge of the village.

Garden Cliff, by contrast, is not a garden in any sense of the word, but a cliff of such size and variety of form that one authority described it as 'The most brilliant and impressive of many cliffs rising from the Severn shore.' Indeed, its very brilliance may well account for its unusual name, for the rocks exposed along its towering face range in colour from red to green, via every conceivable shade of buff and grey, with traces of black and gold thrown in, as it were, for good measure. This gold, incidentally, is actually iron pyrites, also known as fool's gold, and the story goes that round about the turn of the century, some misguided prospectors actually invested money in a hare-brained scheme to mine the stuff!

Fortunately, Garden Cliff withstood this futile threat and when tides permit, we can wander along its foot today, admiring the colourful splendour and keeping a lookout for the fossilized remnants of marine creatures that inhabited the region in past geological epochs. These include ichthyosaurus vertebrae, lung fish jaws, and fish and reptile teeth, all of which have been picked up in recent years. They occur especially after heavy rain has caused sections of the Red Keuper Marl to collapse and so undermine the thin 'Bone bed' layer, which appears as a black band high up on the cliff face.

Back at Strand, where an unclassified road from Westbury leads down to the foot of the cliff, but where parking is strictly limited, a footpath leads over the clifftop to Rodley (see below) from where excellent views across the river — and at suitable times, the Severn Bore — can be enjoyed.

The Dumballs, Rodley

Map 162, GR 745/109. Location sketchmap see page 41. Parking: On verge near Blue Boys Farm, Rodley, along u/c roads from Westbury-on-Severn.

Mainly flat riverbank walking with two alternative circular routes of two-and-a-half and six miles.

Blue Boys Farm stands in isolation at the end of the lane from Rodley — the tip of the long finger of road that stretches to the foot of the peninsula formed by a bold sweep of the Severn between Westbury and Hartland's Hill.

On either side of the farm are the Dumballs — vast expanses of river bank, along which runs the Severn Way Path.

This stretch of the tidal Severn is known as Framilode Passage, after the village directly opposite across the water. This was once a favourite locality for lamprey fishing and many of the fish taken here were supplied, according to ancient custom, to the king, having first been baked in a pie. The local name for the lamprey was pride, or prid, and this seldom-heard word is perpetuated in the name Priding, given to a small hamlet adjoining Framilode over the Severn.

Local people with a good knowledge of the tides are said to have been able to cross the Severn from Priding Point, aiming for the chimneys of the only cottages visible at Rodley. Needless to say, this is definitely not recommended to readers of this book!

Two (dryfoot!) walking options are possible from Blue Boys Farm. Those wishing to take a long walk (about six miles) should cross the stile and turn right to follow the riverside path over Lower Dumball, passing above Garden Cliff to the hamlet of Strand (see page 42). The return route is along lanes via Cleeve and Hayden Farm.

Those preferring a shorter walk

(about two-and-a-half miles) should keep left at the farm and walk over Upper Dumball to meet a track close to the river-widening at Longney Crib. This soon swings inland to meet the Blue Boys Farm approach road at Rodley.

Whichever walk is taken, bird and plant life are both guaranteed to provide interest along the way. Gulls, waders, cormorants and herons are all regulars by the river. As for the plants, a group of naturalists recorded 190 species one day in August, 1989.

Highnam Woods ⊕

Map 162, GR 778/190.
Parking: Small car park off A40, 1 mile W of junction with A48.

300 acres of broadleaved RSPB woodland. Nature trail already established. Further visitor facilities to follow.

The only large surviving tract of woodland between the city of Gloucester and the eastern limits of the Forest of Dean, Highnam is an ancient woodland site (i.e. it has been permanently wooded since Tudor times). Oak comprises most of the canopy layer, although ash is also well established, and wild cherry, poplar and a few stands of silver birch and conifers are also present. The shrub layer is represented by

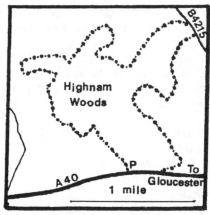

hazel, sallow, dogwood, wild privet and spindle, as well as field maple, some specimens of which are multi-trunked trees of great age.

As befits old oak woodland, there is a rich ground flora with over 200 species positively identified. The spring succession affords a

44

treat for the eye, with primroses and cowslips preparing the way for drifts of bluebells, which together with a scatter of orchids, ensure plenty of colour over the woodland floor throughout April and May.

May is in many ways the high spot of the Highnam year, for it is during the early part of the month that the wood's most notable bird visitor, the nightingale, takes up its summer residence in the dense scrubby areas of the woodland margins. As many as 23 singing males have been recorded in the woods — more than sufficient vocal power to effectively subdue

the ceaseless drone of traffic from the adjacent main road.

Skulking and solitary by habit, the brown and unremarkable-looking nightingale more than compensates for his appearance by the quality and persistence of his voice. What can we add here to the praises heaped upon this song by the poets? Nothing, except to say that the bird can be vocal during the daylight hours too, but at such times the rare quality of its song may be drowned by the combined outpourings of other songsters, such as blackcap, garden warbler, chiffchaff and willow warbler.

Brockeridge Common ⊕

**Map 150, GR 884/382.
Parking: Edge of common on u/c Ripple road, off A38 half-a-mile N of junction 1, M50.**

304-acre private common with public access. Easy walking with some marshy areas.

Brockeridge is a rare Gloucestershire example of what many people think of as a traditional common — an open expanse of scrub-dotted, roughly level ground, its fringes dotted with old cottages, and clumps of woodland beyond to complete the picture.

Sadly though, Brockeridge suffers from that blight of our times — the ever-expanding road network. Not content with seeing it bi-

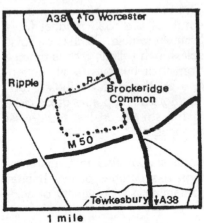

sected by the A38, the planners decided to route the M50 motorway uncomfortably close to the southern edge of the common, and there is no avoiding the constant hum of speeding traffic.

Despite all this, the portion of the

common west of the A38 and on either side of the unclassified road to Ripple is well worth visiting. The northern strip features a tiny willow-lined stream and thickets of sallow and blackthorn. Notice the great patches of mistletoe in the tops of the tallest willows. Along the lane towards Ripple, the stream-side willows are regularly pollarded — lopped at about 10 feet above ground level. Like coppicing, seen elsewhere, pollarding is an ancient craft involving the systematic removal of the tree's top growth to provide a continuous supply of poles. In time, this results in trees with more or less flat-topped boles, the cavities of which often become miniature wild gardens and yield nesting sites for birds.

The main area of the common south of the road is ideal for a leisurely ramble. Patches of gorse splash rich yellow, rabbits emerge from their burrows to sit motionless on the closely-nibbled turf, and horses and ponies graze close to the stream on the south-west boundary.

Botanists will find that this common has patches of wet habitat containing a wide variety of acid-marshland flora — something of a rarity in Gloucestershire.

Woodland, chiefly birch and ash, forms the eastern boundary of the common, with blackthorn thickets ever encroaching from the fringe. Appropriately enough, woodpeckers —both of the green and great-spotted variety — find this area to their liking. Sometimes the yaffling laugh of the one and the mechanical drumming of the other can be heard simultaneously.

Brockeridge Common affords splendid views into Worcestershire, and especially of the full extent of the Malvern range. The great whale-back of Bredon Hill, too, is an impressive sight.

For those wishing to combine a little gentle sightseeing with their visit to Brockeridge Common, a saunter along the lane to Ripple is very worthwhile. This Worcestershire village has a delightful group of crooked timber-framed cottages and a church containing an enchanting collection of misericords — wooden carvings on the undersides of the choirstalls — depicting country activities throughout the year, as recorded by local craftsmen in the 15th century.

The Mythe Railway Reserve, Tewkesbury

**Map 150, GR 887/341.
Parking: Park near nurseries
on A38, N Tewkesbury.
Approach reserve on foot
along Paget's Lane.**

*Length of disused railway
line, now managed as
nature reserve by GTNC.*

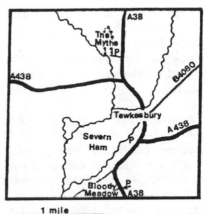

1 mile

The word mythe means a narrow
strip of land between the confluence of two rivers, and Tewkesbury's Mythe is just that, lying as
it does between the Severn and
the Avon. It is a place sure to appeal to railway enthusiasts, having
once formed part of the
Ashchurch — Malvern line, closed
in 1961. It may well attract liter-
ary pilgrims too, for John Moore
wrote of his boyhood exploits
here. But, above all, it exerts a
strong pull on nature lovers, for it
contains grassland, scrub and
remnants of ancient woodland,
and is fringed by water meadows
and an osier bed.

Access to the Mythe is along
Paget's Lane, formerly a section
of the ancient Salt Way linking
Droitwich with the Cotswolds and
the Thames valley. On the right
of the lane stands an old stone
house called King John's Castle,
said to have been built as long
ago as the 12th century as a

hunting lodge for our only
monarch of that name. At the
foot of the lane can be seen the
bricked-up entrance to the Mythe
tunnel, through which trains thun-
dered for a hundred years after its
opening in 1861.

At the top of the embankment
grow several wild service trees,
relics of the former hunting forest. Close by can be found field
maple and spindle, two shrubs
whose leaves, together with those
of the hawthorn, are among the
most colourful in autumn.

From the northern end of the
Mythe, a footpath can be followed to Mythe Hook, providing
good riverside vistas and the
chance to see herons fishing and
cormorants beating their way
above the water.

Severn Ham, Tewkesbury

Map 150, GR 888/326.
Location sketchmap, see
page 47.
Parking: Riverside car park,
Tewkesbury, or nearest
other.

*Traditionally managed 177-
acre hay meadow with
access restricted to public
rights of way. Easy level
walking along grassy paths.*

Lying to the west of the town,
Tewkesbury's Severn Ham is an
expanse of low-lying meadow
land situated between the Severn
and the Mill Avon. It is easily accessible over a footbridge situated
at the end of the lane opposite
the Abbey leading down to the
river. Winter flooding often inun-
dates the entire area, depositing
fertile mud, which in turn, produces flora-rich grassland on
which birds and insects thrive.

The Ham has played a long and
varied role in Tewkesbury's history. Horse races were held on it
until mid-Victorian times, after
which it became the centre for an
annual regatta.

The traditional method of grassland management is still carried
out. This involves a cycle of grazing during the winter months, followed by the growing of a hay
crop subsequently sold by auction.
After haymaking, which must be
concluded by 12th July, the grass
is allowed to grow for a calendar
month before the Aftermath, or
Right of Pasturage, is also auc-
tioned.

Passage over the Ham is therefore restricted to footpaths but
these are clearly defined and enable the walker to undertake a circular stroll directly across the
Ham to the weir on the Severn
and back via Healings Mills.

The short walk is full of atmosphere. Abbey Mill — Abel
Fletcher's to readers of Mrs.
Craik's 'John Halifax, Gentleman'
— provides interest from the
start, as do the views of the town,
dominated by the sturdy Norman
tower of the Abbey itself, described by the late Alec Clifton-
Taylor in his 'Six English Towns'
as 'a grand brooding presence'.
Backs of ancient towns are ofter
as compelling, if not more so,
than the familiar High Street
fronts, and this walk provides a
feast both for the eye and the
mind. Little wonder that local-boy
author, John Moore, was able to
write his 'Portrait of Elmbury',
based on this little town of rivers,
alleyways and history.

Bloody Meadow, Tewkesbury

**Map 150, GR 888/318.
Location sketchmap see page 47.
Parking: Lincoln Green Lane, off A38, half-a-mile S of town centre.**

Town fringe meadow featuring on battle trail. Easy walking.

It may be thought that the gory images associated with a town battle trail have no place in a collection of quiet rural places accessible to the public. However, a section of this trail, known as Bloody Meadow, a narrow, low-lying strip of land south of Tewkesbury, possesses a surprisingly rural character, with sedge warblers chattering in clumps of meadowsweet, and alders and willows providing a picturesque fringe for the western extremity.

The name Bloody Meadow is no gimmick thought up by some enterprising tourist board. "Bloody-furlong" appears as a field name a few years after the fateful day — Saturday, 4th May, 1471 — on which the Lancastrian forces under Queen Margaret of Anjou were routed by the Yorkist army commanded by Edward IV.

As the mounted map at the meadow entrance shows, the exact site of the battle is far from clear. What is certain however, is that hundreds of fleeing Lancastrians were slaughtered close by. A recent planting of red and white thorns commemorates all those slain on both sides. The atmosphere evoked by this simple gesture, together with the chime of the bell from the nearby Norman abbey — in which many of the vanquished sought sanctuary in vain — cannot fail to make a sombre impact.

Those wishing to walk the entire battle trail can do so by following the waymarkings — crossed swords on a rose motif — from Bloody Meadow, along Lower Lode, over the A38, alongside the Swilgate (with superb views of the abbey) and sharp right to reach Abbots Road. The trail then crosses the A38 once more before concluding with field walking back to the start.

Coombe Hill Canal

Map 162, Coombe Hill end, GR 887/273, Wainlode end, GR 849/266.
Parking: Coombe Hill: Lane end from traffic lights at A38/A4019 junction.
Wainlode: Along u/c riverside road linking B4213 and Wainlode Hill.

A two-and-a-half mile disused waterway with a public footpath along virtually its complete length and access at each end. Level walking throughout, but frequently rutted. Impassable during seasonal flooding.

This short, broad canal was dug between the years 1796 and 1797 to enable coal from South Wales and the Forest of Dean to be transported via the River Severn to the expanding town of Cheltenham Spa. As it was cut over the flat, low-lying Chelt valley, no locks were needed, except for the double entrance lock still visible from a public footpath at the meeting of the canal with the Severn at Wainlode.

Winter flooding was a problem from the outset. We can well imagine the ordeal suffered by the horses as they attempted to haul the heavy barges with the towpath churned up into a sea of

squelching mud. But as was so often the case, it was competition — first from a horse-drawn tramway and later from the new railway — that caused the canal to lose trade and to be abandoned finally in 1876.

In 1985, thirty years after the Coombe Hill Canal was designated as a Site of Special Scientific Interest, it was bought by the Gloucestershire Trust for Nature Conservation. Since then, extensive management work has been carried out, including scrub control and selective dredging. This has benefited both aquatic plant and invertebrate life. Yellow iris, common skullcap and purple loosestrife are now well established, together with the graphically-named corky-fruited waterdropwort, while dragonflies and damselflies of several species find conditions to their liking.

50

The visitor exploring the canal from the Coombe Hill end, having driven down to the old wharf, can choose which side of the canal on which to walk. From the footbridge carrying the footpath from Leigh to Apperley however, there is a path on the north bank only for the remaining mile or so to Wainlode.

Churchdown Hill

Map 162, GR 882/188. Parking: At top of lane signposted 'Church and Water Works' from Churchdown Green.

Network of footpaths giving access to church-crowned hilltop offering mixture of city and country views.

Like Robinswood Hill, three and a half miles to the south-west, Churchdown Hill is an outlier of the main Cotswold range, stranded now — a precious oasis — in a sprawling desert of concrete, brick and tarmac. It lacks the height of Robinswood — a mere 154 metres at its summit, compared with 198 — but more than compensates for that shortcoming in possessing an ancient church, perched on a rocky outcrop overlooking Churchdown village.

It sounds reasonable to suppose that the hill got its name from this church but experts on such matters assure us otherwise. Churchdown is in fact a hybrid word, made up from the Celtic 'crouco' and the Old English 'dun', both of which meant hill. The alternative name, Chosen Hill, does not appear to have been adopted until the 16th century.

In fact the word oasis, used earlier in a figurative sense, has a degree of literal truth too, when applied to Churchdown Hill. There is a record of water being piped from a spring on the hill to supply the village as long ago as the 12th century, while at the present day, three underground reservoirs play a vital role in providing water for Gloucester and Cheltenham.

But it is St. Bartholmew's Church that provides the main attraction on this windswept hilltop. Why did the people of Churchdown, 800 or more years ago, decide to build their church high above the village? Predictably, legend has it

51

that this was the work of the Devil who, determined to deprive the villagers of their Mass, carried off the load of stones from the church building site on the lower slopes, and dumped them on high. Undeterred, the folk of Churchdown erected their church at this very spot, a rocky eminence of weather-resistant marlstone. Even so, repairs and reinforcement have been needed to shore up the building over the centuries and more such work will soon be needed, judging by a jagged crack visible in the outer walls.

Leaving the churchyard, with its quaint old verger's cottage and garden close by, we find a wide choice of well-marked footpaths criss-crossing the hilltop. One of these, near Yew Tree Cottage, leads to the triangulation pillar on the hill's highest point, from which impressive views of Gloucester, the Cotswold ridge and more distant landmarks can be enjoyed.

The hill's southern flanks are well timbered. Mature oak and ash grow here, interspersed with a few gnarled old field maples and a scatter of hawthorn scrub. To the east, a clump of stately Scots pines defy the elements, while the lower slopes towards Hucclecote are clad with patches of gorse and bracken. Below, on every side, the world rushes by. The cacophany of this constant turmoil is carried upwards to mingle with the peace of Churchdown Hill's bird song and rustling leaves, but its impact is lessened and put in true perspective on these green and pleasant slopes.

St. Bartholemew's Church

52

Robinswood Hill Country Park ⊕

**Map 162, GR 840/150.
Parking: Official car park off
Reservoir Road, Tuffley, off
A38/A417 roundabout.**

*City-fringe country park set
on steep hillside. Toilets.*

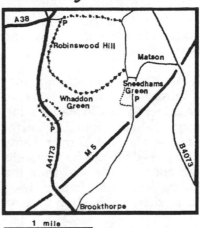

Although an outlier of the
Cotswolds, Robinswood Hill is
unique in that it lies wholly within
the boundary of the city of
Gloucester. Designated as a
Country Park early in the 1970s,
it has a dry ski slope, a BMX
track and the predictable golf
course, plus a visitor centre and
waymarked trails.

All this may sound somewhat off-
putting to those seeking access to
the peace and tranquillity of the
Gloucestershire countryside yet
there is still much to commend
Robinswood. Its geology in particular is worth investigation for the
Tuffley Quarry on the hill's western flank reveals the finest inland
exposure of Middle Lias strata to
be seen in the whole of England,
and is not surprisingly designated
as a Site of Special Scientific Interest. These rocks are rich in fossils and a fine collection can be
seen in Gloucester City Museum.

Robinswood's highest point,
known locally as The Camel's
Hump, stands at 650 feet above
sea-level and from here can be

seen splendid views of the city
and its dominating cathedral
tower. Additionally, there are excellent contrasting vistas of the
Cotswold heights around
Painswick and Haresfield Beacons, the Sharpness Canal and
the Vale of Severn. The constant
drone of the city and the M5 motorway may be ever-present but
the views and fresh breezes more
than compensate for the climb.

The natural history of
Robinswood provides further in-
centive to linger on this city-fringe
hilltop. Beech and oak woodland
is augmented by plantings of
birch, larch and wild cherry and
some old thorns have grown into
venerable trees. Scrub-encroachment on grassland areas requires
regular control to safeguard the
limestone flora, which includes
primroses, cowslips and spotted

orchids. Another attraction is provided by patches of wetland. These comprise ponds and springs which once served to supply the city's needs but are now valuable breeding habitat for newts (all three British species), frogs and toads. Grass snakes also favour these damp localities.

It is hardly surprising that Robinswood Hill has featured prominently in Gloucester's history. Called originally Mattes Knowle, after the Norman family who owned the nearby manor, its present name derived from the Robins family who farmed sheep on its slopes in the 16th century.

Brickmaking and iron-smelting came and went many years ago, while the hill witnessed a brief interlude of national history in 1643, when King Charles stayed at Matson House while his army laid siege to Gloucester.

Today, despite Gloucester's encroachment from every other direction, it is still possible to leave (or approach) Robinswood by footpaths from the south. For walkers, these paths serve to maintain Robinswood's link with the Cotswolds, of which the hill formed part in past geological time.

Whaddon Green

Map 162, GR 834/138. Location sketchmap, see page 53.
Parking: Village street adjacent to common, on A4173, Gloucester — Stroud road.

Traditional, flat village green, unfortunately bisected by busy main road.

Can there really be two extensive greens, scarcely a mile apart, tucked in between the M5 and the southern tentacles of Gloucester? And can they possibly be connected by a meandering country footpath, picking its way over fields in the lee of a fine hilltop, one of the most distinctive outliers of the Cotswold Range? The answers, unlikely as it may seem,

are yes on both counts, the greens being Whaddon and Sneedham's (see below).

Whaddon's green, two surprisingly spacious stretches of open grassland on either side of the A4173, retains a traditional village green appearance in spite of everything that progress — in the twin shapes of the building brick and the motor car — continues to throw at it.

Whaddon is a tiny village — a thirteenth century church, a school, a few houses and scattered farms — with the smaller western half of its green serving as an effective cushion/barrier against the frantic rush close by. The green is complete with pond, though virtually impossible to approach on account of the elm scrub which fringes it. An old timber-framed cottage nearby completes the picture.

The main feature of the larger, eastern part of the green is a planting of oaks screened by quicker-growing poplars. There is a scatter of other trees, too — commemorative specimens, mostly oak, hornbeam and horse chestnut — while the eastern boundary is fringed with veteran willows, full of character and affording plenty of sites for hole-nesting birds.

The green's southern boundary is defined by a stream, lush in summer with reed mace and willow herb, beyond which is an old hedge consisting of oak, ash, hawthorn, blackthorn, field maple, dogwood, elm and dog rose — a splendid and long-established mixture.

As well as Robinswood Hill's alluring slopes close at hand, and reached by footpath, the view takes in May Hill and the eastern reaches of the Forest of Dean.

Within living memory, Whaddon Green was grazed both by sheep and horses. However, increasing traffic caused the change of use to one of hay-production.

Sneedham's Green $\oplus$

Map 162, GR 847/144. Location sketchmap, see page 53. Parking: Verge parking along u/c Matson — Brookthorpe road.

Another traditional green, but one whose rural position enables long-established farming practices to continue.

Despite the close proximity of the M5 and Matson's high density housing estates, Sneedham's Green, like that of Whaddon (see above), with which it is connected by footpath, is surprisingly unmarred by the march of time. Beyond the buzzing motorway, a wide sweep of open country beckons, stretching away to the wooded hills of Cranham, Painswick and Harescombe.

But rural Gloucestershire starts here, on this wide level green with its scatter of smallholdings and cottages. The winding lane, after dipping from crossing the motorway, reverts to its former unfenced state and allows grazing sheep to wander unimpeded as did their forebears in times past. May this unhurried pastoral tempo long remain, bringing, as it does, a touch of sanity to a rootless, restless world.

Frampton-on-Severn Village Green | ⊕

Map 162, GR 750/080.
Parking: In car park by post office in village which lies on B4071, reached from A38 one mile S of junction with A419.

A flat 22-acre village green with good paths providing easy walking.

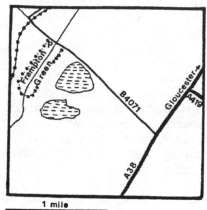

1 mile

Those who doubt whether big can ever be linked compatably with beautiful should visit Frampton. For here can be found not only Gloucestershire's largest village green, but also one of the county's most delightful settings.

To be honest, the northern end of Frampton, lining the road to Saul, reflects the workaday nature of many other Severnside settlements. But those turning left on approaching the village from the A38 direction cannot fail to be impressed by what lies before them — a vast expanse of grass, fringed with gracious buildings, all beautifully maintained, and the whole embodying everyone's ideal of what a village should look like.

Can this first impression withstand closer scrutiny? To find out, leave the car in the small car park and see for yourself. If you are a cricket lover and choose a summer afternoon, the chances are that you won't get beyond this northern extremity of the green.

For on these occasions, the game played in such a perfect setting may well prove irresistible.

Other times to avoid (or to choose, according to taste) are Easter Monday, when elver-eating competitions are held, and the Saturday in August reserved for Frampton Feast, a traditional event featuring a deer roast and other festivities.

At other times, Frampton Green can be seen in its true state, un-adorned except by its three rush-fringed ponds, its horse chestnuts and its wild flowers, all overlooked by a charming group of stone, mellow brick and timber-framed buildings. Outstanding among these is Manor Farm, once the manor house of the Cliffords, and supposedly the birthplace of the legendary Jane, better known as Fair Rosamund.

To many, this green is Rosamund's Green, a reminder of the village lord's beautiful daughter who became Henry II's mistress and who, after being poisoned by the jealous Queen Eleanor, was buried at Godstow nunnery, near Oxford. To others, the green has associations with later Clifford ladies — the 19th century artists whose collection of flower paintings lay forgotten in an attic in Frampton Court for 130 years until their discovery and publication in 1985 as 'The Frampton Flora'.

To the east of the village — and its green — are two large lakes formed by the flooding of worked-out gravel pits. A network of sign-posted public footpaths gives access to this valuable bird habitat, with its resident population of Canada geese, mallard, teal, tufted duck and great-crested grebe. Cormorants and herons find the fishing rewarding, while in winter, the residents are joined by flocks of wigeon, pochard, pintail and shoveler ducks.

Gloucester & Sharpness Canal

Map 162, GR 668/029.
Parking: At T-junction on B4066 beyond Wanswell, turn right for N end of Sharpness Docks. Road swings sharp left to cross old railway and canal bridges. Park as near as possible to Severn Way Path.

A canal-towpath walk, level throughout, to Purton — two miles each way or beyond.

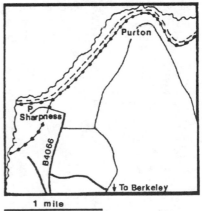

1 mile

The Gloucester and Sharpness is Gloucestershire's only working canal, and at 16 miles in length and 90 feet wide, was the largest in England until the construction of the Manchester Ship Canal.

Formerly known as the Berkeley Canal, owing to the original intention for it to enter the Severn at Berkeley Pill, this remarkable waterway was opened in 1827 after no less than 33 years of wrangling and delay. Its building almost halved the distance boats had to travel to reach Gloucester, and it was designed to carry vessels of up to 1,000 tons, with no locks except at Sharpness and Gloucester.

The port of Sharpness has two docks — Old Dock, opened at the same time as the canal, and New Dock, constructed in 1874. Good views can be had of Old Docks's tidal basin, lock house and the original entrance lock from the Severn, at the start of the walk.

A short distance along the towpath can be seen the abutment of the former Severn rail bridge, which was built in 1879 to connect Sharpness with the Gloucester-Chepstow line near Lydney. The bridge was demolished in 1969 after having been badly damaged by colliding barges.

But by far the most fascinating industrial relics seen from the canal towpath are the rotting hulks of old sailing vessels beached along the Ridge Sand. Known as trows, these boats bore the brunt of the task of transporting cargoes to and from Gloucester in the era before engine-driven vessels rendered them obsolete.

At Purton, where there is a choice of two pubs for refreshment, can be seen the first of five distinctive canal bridge-keeper's houses, stuccoed and complete with Doric columns, that are a feature of the waterway.

This stretch of the canal, hugging the Severn Bank, affords good bird-watching possibilities. Depending on the state of the tide, a range of gulls and waders can be observed, together with herons, cormorants and the handsome black, white and chestnut shelduck, resembling a goose as it flies off with slow wing-beats.

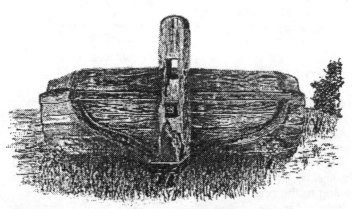

Severn trow hulk

Whitcliff Park, Ham

Map 162, GR 677/979.
Parking: Roadside verge, adjacent junction of B4509 with u/c Clapton and Bevington road, three-quarters of a mile S of Berkeley.

Public footpath providing linear walk across private deer park. Access over ladder stile.

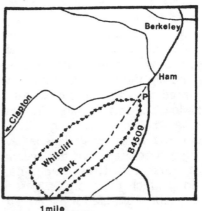

1 mile

An ancient walled deer park crossed by a public footpath is by no means a commonplace feature in Gloucestershire. Whitcliff Park, which extends south-westwards from Ham, near Berkeley, to the Avon border, is just that, so although the visitor must either retrace steps or embark on a circular four mile ramble via Bevington and Comeley Farms and back along the minor road, it seems worthy of inclusion.

Park on the verge by the road junction and follow the waymarked footpath up a field. Good views of the Severn estuary and of Berkeley nuclear power station, now being de-commissioned, can be had to the right. Enter the park up steps over the wall. Pass the ornate lodge cottage on the left and climb the clearly-defined track leading towards an avenue of trees ahead.

There is no missing the fine herds of fallow deer, in the Autumn each watched over by a single male (buck), distinguished by the flattened antlers in the form of a broad curved plate from which several points project. The colour of this species of deer varies widely, although a prominent dark line down the centre of the back, is characteristic, as are the roundish white spots on the sides during the summer months. Bucks take six years to develop a full head of antlers, which are shed each May, a few weeks before the young are born. New antler growth is complete by the end of September and in the following month, the bucks challenge one another for the does by a ritual clashing of antlers which, though often prolonged, seldom results in serious harm to the combatants.

Whitcliff's history as a deer park dates from the thirteenth century, when the then Lord Berkeley seized the land on top of the long wooded ridge and banished the peasants who had hitherto grazed their livestock there. The enclosing wall came much later, no doubt replacing an earlier boundary, possibly a wattle fence. Also gone are the fine trees that once graced the scene; a few old oaks, hollow and mis-shapen, cling on, together with a scattering of London planes and miscellaneous evergreen conifers, but the avenue of horse chestnuts and limes along which the footpath passes is a poor substitute for the ancient woodland.

The romantically-inclined may wish to ponder on the possibility that the rotting trunks strewn over the park may have borne witness in their heyday to the hunting exploits of Queen Elizabeth I. It was in 1573 that the Queen, accompanied by her friend Robert Dudley, enjoyed a day's slaughtering of Lord Berkeley's deer. Tradition has it that the Lord, who was absent at the time, was reduced to impotent fury on his return.

Today, the deer park, although a mere shadow of its former splendour, offers a quiet country walk, bird song and the chatter of jackdaws providing the only distractions from precious tranquillity.

Fallow deer buck

The Cotswolds

The Gloucestershire Cotswolds fall into five fairly distinctive physical divisions. Briefly, these are the scarp face, extending south-westwards from Mickleton in the far north of the county down to Wotton-under-Edge; the wide upland country between Winchcombe and Chipping Campden; the open wold landscape stretching eastwards from the scarp and including the Stow, Bourton and Northleach areas; the deep, wooded valleys of the Stroud-Nailsworth region; and the gentle southern wold county around Cirencester, Bibury and Tetbury.

Desirable though it seemed to arrange the selected sites according to these divisions, in practice it proved impractical. Instead, to give this, the largest section of the book, a simple and easy-to-follow structure, I have arranged the Cotswolds in three straightforward bands — north (everywhere north of a line from Birdlip to Northleach); central (places south of the above line and north of a similar line from Stroud to Bibury); and south (south of the Stroud to Bibury line). Even with this method of division, some zig-zagging is unavoidable, as those with a working knowledge of the region will readily appreciate.

The chosen sites are chiefly hills, open commons and woods, supplemented by a scatter of village greens. The mix is enriched in the southern section however, by the inclusion of Cirencester Park, the Cotswold Water Park, the Thames-Severn Canal and Westonbirt Arboretum. Inevitably, shortage of space has imposed severe restrictions on my choice. No doubt readers will enjoy finding their own sites — and possibly asking how on earth I could have omitted such obvious gems from my final selection!

Almsbury barn, Sudeley

Dover's Hill, Chipping Campden | ⊕

**Map 151, GR 137/397.
Parking: Official car park off
u/c Chipping Campden —
Weston Subedge road.**

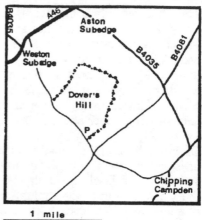

1 mile

*184 acres of NT-owned
hilltop at northern
extremity of Cotswolds.
Special disabled gate and
path to topograph and
viewpoint.*

Dover's Hill is all that remains of
a 500-acre common known as
Kingcombe Plain, the greater part
of which was enclosed early in the
19th century.

But for the public-spirited vision
of the artist F.L. Griggs a century
later, this last fragment of north
Cotswold hilltop would have been
lost too — this time to developers
wishing to build a luxury hotel on
the site.

It was in 1929 that the National
Trust finally purchased Dover's
Hill for the nation. Today, it attracts thousands of visitors, most
of whom are content to stroll
from their cars to the topograph
and back again, taking with them
a fleeting idea of the view and
possibly a vague mental impression of the man whose name the
hill perpetuates, gained from his
picture on the collecting box near
the car park. This man was
Robert Dover, a local lawyer, who

in 1612, founded the so-called
'Cotswold Olympicks' with the
blessing of James I. He is shown
dressed in clothes that once be-
longed to the King himself,
crowned with a feathered hat and
mounted on a white horse.

The event opened with the firing
of cannon, mounted on the twin
towers of a portable wooden castle, after which Dover rode out to
be greeted by the applause of the
gathered multitude.

The games were held on the
Thursday and Friday after Whit-
sun, and included cudgel-play,
wrestling, shin-kicking, pitching
the bar, throwing the iron ham-
mer and hare coursing, with a few
sedentary activities such as chess
and card games, played in tents.

Apart from a temporary suppression during the Commonwealth period, the 'Olympicks' were held regularly until the mid-19th century, by which time they had degenerated into scenes of drunken brawling involving gangs of navvies working on the nearby Mickleton railway tunnel. This led to their discontinuation in 1853, followed by the enclosure of much of the common.

A modified version of the games, held on the Friday evening after Spring Bank Holiday Monday, has flourished since its revival for the Festival of Britain in 1951, and culminates in a torchlight procession down the hill to Chipping Campden.

The creation of the Cotswold Way has increased the popularity of Dover's Hill, for the route sweeps up to the escarpment and in so doing takes in the splendid views for which it is justly noted. The scarp at this point swings north-eastwards in a great arc

above a vast amphitheatre. After identifying the prominent landmarks visible from the topograph, walk along the rim to the triangulation pillar and as far as Bold Gap, from which a waymarked path descends to Lynches Wood. A nature trail, indicated by numbered oak posts, has been laid out in the wood and descriptive leaflets are available from a dispenser in the car park.

Those wishing to walk further afield can follow the Cotswold Way from here. For Chipping Campden, a footpath leads south-eastwards to reach Hoo Lane, while those who prefer to aim in the direction of Broadway, need to follow roads at first to reach the Kiftsgate Stone. Alternatively, a delightful walk can be taken in a north-westerly direction from the topograph towards Weston Subedge and/or Saintbury, two villages brimming over with interest and comparatively unscathed by the tourist tide.

Broadwell Green

Map 163, GR 205/274. Parking: In village lying on u/c road linking A429 and A436, 2 miles NE Stow-on-the-Wold.

3-acre stream-fringed green in picture-postcard north Cotswold village.

This pleasant village green, referred to as No Man's Land in the county greens' register, was given

to the village fairly recently, as can be seen from an inscribed limestone block, complete with surrounding seat: 'In memory of Lord Ashton of Hyde (1901-1983) of Broadwell Hill, by whose generosity this green can be enjoyed by all'.

No place could be more aptly named. Springs and wells abound in and around the village, giving rise to the ford at the eastern end of the green and helping to swell the infant River Evenlode, wriggling its sinuous way southwards, a mere mile away to the east.

From any one of the seats arranged around the green, the attractive grouping of cottages, farms and the Fox Inn cannot fail to give pleasure. Looking west beyond the rooftops, the rim of the beech-topped wolds completes the picture.

The green itself, mown and manicured, offers little more than daisies and dandelions but the stream along its northern fringe more than makes up for this deficiency. Here, under the willows in spring and early summer, are colourful clumps of forget-me-not, herb robert, wild iris, water figwort and pungent water mint, while a mat of liverworts encrusts the stonework.

The willows themselves reward close inspection, for their split and contorted trunks serve as hosts to innumerable other trees and flowering plants. One such veteran has a sycamore growing from within its breached trunk, as well as lusty saplings of elm, elder, hawthorn and yew, all well established higher up.

And what child can resist a water splash? The ford is crossed only by local traffic and supervision from the adjacent green is easy. A further attraction for the studiously inclined is St. Paul's Church, with its wool-bale tombs in the churchyard. An excellent, concise village history is obtainable inside the church.

Bledington Green & Nature Reserve | ⊕

Map 163, GR 247/227. Location sketchmap see page 62.
Parking: In village, which lies on B4450 Stow — Chipping Norton road.

Two contrasting open spaces in a distinctive Cotswold fringe village.

The village of Bledington, in the valley of the River Evenlode, is the proud possessor of a village green across which a tiny stream flows. This, with its reedy ditches, is the haunt of a flotilla of ducks of dubious pedigree, which demand food from the unwary visitor amd complain loudly if it is not forthcoming. Approaching round a blind corner, the motorist is warned of their presence by an 'official' sign — which is just as well, for on summer days, the ducks often take their siesta in the middle of the road!

Bledington Green is in fact several small greens around which are grouped a collection of elegant houses of Cotswold stone. The gardens of some of these are fenced with stone slabs held together by iron brackets — a feature found in other villages in the Evenlode and Windrush valleys.

For those seeking refreshment, the King's Head Inn also stands close by and there are swings and a seesaw for the children.

Climbing from the green past more attractive houses is Church Street, leading to the beautiful church of St. Leonard, famous for its Perpendicular windows and stained glass. The long distance footpath, the Oxfordshire Way, passes close by on its way to Bourton-on-the-Water.

A short distance from Bledington along the Stow road is a 6-acre nature reserve created by the parish council. Essentially a strip of verge bordering the bridleway to Lower Oddington, it lies between ancient hedges and includes plantings of oak, rowan and cherry. Also of interest are some old willows and some even older ashes. The nature reserve includes a stream crossed by a quaint little bridge, and extends as far as the bed of the old railway track all that remains of the Kingham-Stow-Bourton line.

Many may wish to walk further — as far perhaps as the lovely little church of St. Nicholas, alone in Oddington Ashes, over a couple of meandering miles distant. But beware — squelchy ruts and tormenting insects await! Wellies can cope with the first of these hazards, while extra-strong repellant might just make some impression on the other.

Tatwell Green (The Tattle), Westcote

Map 163, GR 222/205. Location sketchmap see page 63. Parking: Church Westcote village which lies on u/c Westcote — Idbury road off A424.

Sloping, roughly-maintained 3-acre green overlooking Oxfordshire Cotswolds.

This tiny green fringes the road connecting the two parts of Westcote, on the exposed, north-facing ridge above the Evenlode valley, parallel to the Stow-Burford road.
Bordered by a stone wall and mixed hedges, this green receives none of the manicuring treatment usually reserved for village greeens. In other words, it resembles a miniature common, with in-

termittent grazing, while in early spring the blackthorn thicket at the eastern end is a frothy mass of blossom, which gives rise to bumper sloe crops in due season.

The views from this lofty perch are impressive, to say the least. The Cotswold-fringe country of Oxfordshire stretches away to the Evenlode, with Kingham church almost in line with that of Gloucestershire's Bledington, and Churchill's proud tower — a scaled-down copy of Magdalen's celebrated edifice — prominent away to the north-east.

A chequerwork of fields and hedges fills the middle distance — typical Cotswold dip-slope landscape, yet when viewed from here somehow seeming quintessentially English — the 'landscape plotted and pieced — field, fallow and plough', of the poet.

Still on the subject of ploughing, Westcote was one of the last villages in the Cotswolds in which the old open-field system of farming persisted. The land between the village and the A424 was until recent years cultivated in long strips separated by baulks of unploughed ground for access.

Those wishing to combine an exploratory walk with their visit to Tatwell Green can leave the common along the footpath to Nether Westcote, which has a quiet pub, and then, if so desired, follow the lane over the Oxfordshire border to Idbury, famous as the birthplace in 1927, of J.W. Robertson Scott's 'The Countryman' magazine. Scott's former house stands prominently in this tiny hilltop village with the words of Virgil: *'O more than happy countryman if he but knew his good fortune'* — still in place over the door.

Wyck Rissington Green

Map 163, GR 190/217.
Location sketchmap see page 63.
Parking: Wyck Rissington village, one-and-a-half miles E of A429
near Bourton-on-the-Water.

6-acre village green lying on both sides of minor road in attractive village setting.

Spacious village greens are scarce in Gloucestershire and especially in the east Cotswolds. Wyck Rissington's, therefore, is all the more

remarkable especially as its fringes are dotted with 17th and 18th century cottages built in the traditional style of local stone, giving it the appearance of the kind of village green often extolled in rural literature, but all too seldom found, even in the heart of a pastoral landscape.

To perfect the picture, the green comes complete with village pond, and is lined with fine horse chestnut trees.

Wyck Rissington lies in the Windrush valley, little more than a meandering footpath mile to the east of the groping tentacles of Bourton-on-the-Water. In fact, it is the enchanting little River Dikler, a tributary of the Windrush, that picks its way through the nearby meadows, which being low-lying, are rich in damp-loving wild flowers.

Gravel extraction in the 1960s and 1970s gave rise to a series of lakes in this valley (see Bourton Lakes), and these are passed by walkers following the Oxfordshire Way. This long-distance footpath which descends from Wyck Beacon on the watershed between the Windrush and Evenlode valleys, enters Wyck Rissington through its churchyard and proceeds via the green on its way to Bourton.

St. Lawrence's church at the southern end of the village, is well worth seeing. The composer Gustav Holst was organist here and later, one of its rectors, Harry Cheales, built a maze in his garden following a vision. The maze, like the rector, has gone but the traveller is reminded of both by a memorial located in the churchyard wall.

Bourton-on-the-Water Lakes

Map 163 and location sketchmap page 63.
Parking: Three possible starting points — Rissington Bridge, Bourton-on-the Water, GR 179/198, Rissington Mill Lane, Little Rissington, GR 184/197, and Wyck Rissington village, GR 188/219.

Chain of privately-owned lakes linked by network of public footpaths.

The village of Bourton-on-the-Water gets the latter part of its name from its situation on the River Windrush, but anyone unfamiliar with its origins could be excused for imagining that the chain of lakes round its southern margin were responsible.

In fact, these lakes are comparative newcomers to the Windrush valley, having been created by the flooding of gravel workings which were discontinued during the 1970s. They have been landscaped and put to varying uses — some serving as a trout farm, others being stocked for angling, while others, being comparatively undisturbed, provide valuable wetland habitat for wildlife.

All these lakes are privately owned but a network of public footpaths enables walkers to explore them. There is a choice of starting points, depending on how long a walk is desired. The best of these for circular walks (all on OS 163) are Rissington Bridge (179/198), Rissington Mill Lane (184/197) and Wyck Rissington Green (188/219).

Although this artificial lakeland supports a wide variety of flowers and insects, bird life provides the main attraction. There is a marked seasonal variation in wetland bird populations. During the spring and summer months, good views can be had of such breeding species as coot, moorhen, great crested grebe, little grebe, mallard and tufted duck. Larger birds — mute swan, Canada goose and heron, as well as several species of gulls — may be present in varying numbers, while overhead, myriads of insects attract great numbers of swallows, martins and swifts.

From Autumn until March, the lakes provide ideal winter quarters for large numbers of ducks, including pochard and wigeon. The birds float in large rafts well away from the banks, in marked contrast to the kingfisher and dipper, two other regular visitors noted for their rapid flight low over the water.

Guiting Wood

Map 163, GR 083/261. Parking: Small car park (084/259) alongside gated road to Kineton, off u/c Winchcombe Guiting Power road.

Extensive private woodland crossed by several public footpaths, some of which link with quiet minor roads. Some steep gradients and wet patches after rain.

'I cannot believe that there is another such wood as Guiting in England, not another at any rate whose magic is of so aerial, transporting a quality'.
So wrote that doyen of modern country authors, H.J. Massingham, in his book 'Shepherd's Country', published in 1938. Half a century plus of change — especially the replacement of old hardwood trees by conifers — has impinged inevitably on this fine

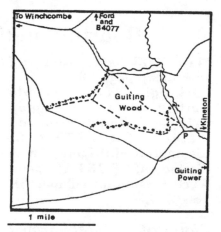

wood since then, yet amazingly, a little of the magic still clings.

A good deal of Guiting Wood's appeal stems from its setting. It dominates a sweep of wold country between Sudeley Park on the west, the Upper Windrush valley on the east, with ruins of the once-splendid Hailes Abbey to the north and the site of the lost medieval village of Roel to the south.

Sharpening the focus, we see that a tributary of the infant Windrush carves its tortuous little valley round the wood's northern and eastern perimeters, while an ancient drovers' road, Campden Lane, clips its western extremity at a crossroads rejoicing in the name of Deadmanbury Gate.

And in case all this fails to lure the curious explorer, two more abandoned medieval villages — Pinnock and Castlett — can be traced close by. The sinister-sounding Black John's Pool lies by the wood's southern fringe, while deep within its heart are the remains of a prehistoric tumulus.

Tragically, the ancient oak- and ash-dominated heart of Guiting Wood that won Massingham's lavish praise was ruthlessly cleared in the years following his visit. The mixed conifers that replaced these fine trees are a poor substitute, and it is doubtful how many of 400-plus flowering plants and 60 species of mosses once recorded still remain. Certainly, carpets of bluebells are rolled out in welcome every spring, and the oddly distinctive herb paris still blooms, as do the early-flowering green hellebore and the graceful lilac-coloured wood vetch by the woodland edge. Of the others, one suspects, but a few stragglers manage to linger on.

Take any one of the main public footpaths through Guiting Wood and you will be sure to come across a stout round-topped stone, resembling an old milestone, set at a fork in the path. Peer closely and you will decipher the words 'No public road here', incised into the stone, a reminder of the time when the wood, now the property of a forestry company, was owned by an Oxford college. At least, these moss-covered stones still serve to keep the walker on the right track!

By following the path over the stile to the left of the cottage visible from the car park, it is possible to walk through Guiting Wood, emerging at the northwest corner. From here, there is a choice between returning via woodland paths or back by the minor road to the right, which eventually follows the Windrush tributary in switchback fashion along its delightful wooded valley.

Cleeve Common

Map 163, GRs 986/270, 994/248.
Parking and access: Cleeve Hill, car parks off B4632 Cheltenham — Winchcombe road, or Radio masts, u/c road from A40 via Whittington.

A vast open common with glorious views, invigorating walking, historical and wildlife interest. Fairly level walking from radio masts. Toilets at Cleeve Hill

To the lover of the open air, Cleeve Common is the jewel in the Cotswold crown. Consider the facts: Over 1300 acres covering some three square miles. By far the largest common in Gloucestershire and, rising to 1083 feet above sea level, not only the highest hilltop in the county but also the highest area in lowland England east of the River Severn. Add to all this the fact that the common is scheduled as a Grade One SSSI on account of its natural beauty and wildlife content and it becomes clear that this is one of the most outstanding open spaces in Gloucestershire.

The word cleeve — derived from the Old English for cliff — appears several times in association with other local names on the map. This leaves the two Cleeves we are concerned with here — Cleeve Common, the correct name for the high ground itself, and Cleeve Cloud, which is the precipitous edge along the western rim of the common beloved by rock-climbers, and which catches the eye from a considerable distance westwards.

Being so close to Cheltenham, Cleeve Common has for a century or so at least, been a townsman's playground. The horse-racing which once took place here, long ago moved to Prestbury Park, but the common is still a mecca for riders, golfers, rock-climbers, kite- and model plane flyers, not to mention walkers, many of whom are following the Cotswold Way.

Yet despite all this use, Cleeve Common retains an atmosphere of lofty spaciousness totally unlike any other part of the Cotswolds. Wandering over its vast expanse, the discerning walker comes upon a tiny stream trickling down a ravine-like valley to a disused sheepwash pool; long-abandoned quarries with patches of scree blanketed by limestone polypody fern; an area of gorse, intermingled with heather, reminiscent of a Welsh mountainside; a prehistoric earthwork that in its heyday must have been virtually impregnable and many, many more features, natural and man-made, that stir the curiosity and feed the imagination.

Although technically not on the common, a visit to the area would not be complete without including **Belas Knap long barrow (GR 021/253)**. This Neolithic burial chamber shares with Hetty Pegler's Tump (see Coaley Wood) the distinction of being the finest example of its kind in the Cotswolds. Perched at over 900 feet above sea level, its stonework was painstakingly restored in the 1930s after successive excavations had left it in a deplorable state. Altogether the remains of some thirty burials were discovered and an assortment of grave goods, some of which can be seen in Cheltenham museum.

Thanks to seasonal sheep-grazing over the years, Cleeve Common is recognized as one of the finest botanical sites in the Cotswolds. At least 230 species of plants have been recorded, 50 of which are uncommon at either county or national level.

To many, Cleeve Common is essentially a viewpoint, and rightly so, for it is the finest in the Cotswolds. From the car park at the summit of Cleeve Hill, it is but a short climb to the panorama dial at 1040 feet above sea level, from which the views beyond the silver thread of the Severn and the Forest of Dean into Wales are unforgettable on a clear day. However, those wishing to set foot on the highest point in Gloucestershire must stride out southwards to the triangulation pillar just beyond the radio masts, which surprisingly stands at 1083 feet.

Belas Knapp

71

Nottingham Hill & Longwood Common

Map 163, GR 984/279.
Parking: On edge of Longwood Common, about three-quarters of a mile along u/c road off B4632 almost opposite High Roost Inn.

Good scenic walking over undulating terrain to west of Cleeve Common.
Includes open common, woodland and remains of ancient fort.

Such is the dominance of Cleeve Common, commanding the high ground for miles around, that it is easy to overlook the fine promontary of Nottingham Hill, thrusting northwards from the main Cleeve ridge and rising 915 feet above sea level.

To see Nottingham Hill — and the ramparts of the prehistoric fort built upon it — it is best to park on near the viewpoint (symbol on map) and climb to the hill via Bushcombe Wood. In this way, both scenery and early man's constructional achievements can best be appreciated, and a short yet bracing walk enjoyed over somewhat uneven, but hardly difficult terrain.

Longwood Common lies on the opposite side of the lane from the farm of the same name. Climb

the well-worn track through hawthorn scrub. A few strides are sufficient to bring fine scenery into view westwards, stretching in a vast sweep from the quarried flanks of Cleeve Hill to include Cheltenham, with its racecourse in the foreground, before fading away into the distant Vale of Gloucester.

Longwood is a hillside common and as such has been quarried for centuries, giving it a hump-and-hollow surface beloved of limestone flowers and the butterflies that thrive upon them. Here grow carline, woolly and nodding thistles, salad burnet and scabious. Small mammals too, lurk in the thick grassy tussocks and beneath the ruined walls, unseen by man but vulnerable to hanging kestrels the moment they scurry over the sparse turf. There are also ancient anthills, well marked by rabbits, which in the absence of sheep are instrumental in keeping the grass grazed.

Bushcombe Wood is predominantly old hazel coppice, with a carpet of dog's mercury underfoot. Ash and silver birch have also colonised the wood, together with crab apple trees that yield heavily in good seasons.

The track climbs steadily to leave the wood over a stile beyond which Woolstone Hill, its flank scarred with old field boundaries, rises up directly ahead. Over its shoulder peeps Bredon Hill, the poets' favourite, belonging to Worcestershire yet an outlier of the Gloucestershire Cotswolds. Away westwards, the Malverns rear up majestically as ever, a vast backdrop.beneath which the sturdy tower of Tewkesbury Abbey is dwarfed into the insignificance of a tossed-away plaything.

To the right rise the earthworks of the prehistoric camp, thought to have been Iron Age until recent times, when the discovery of a hoard of Bronze Age tools revealed its earlier origin. Later, this 120-acre hilltop, with its 10 foot-high inner bank was used by the Romans as a signalling station.

Yellow arrows denote the route through Gotherington Wood, in which larch serves as cover for young beeches. Beyond, as the path swings right to cross Nottingham Hill's flat summit back to the start, the wooded outliers of Alderton and Dumbleton present a last memorable vista of the meeting of vale and wold.

Leckhampton Hill

**Map: 163, GR 949/189.
Parking: Official car park, Daisybank Road, off B4070, about 2 miles S Cheltenham.**

275-acre, Borough-owned quarried hill. Outstanding geological and wildlife interest. Of special appeal to industrial archaeologists. Superb views and very steep gradients.

'The ridges of Leckhampton Hill are some of the boldest and most lofty of the Cotswolds; they are broken more precipitously, and exhibit a greater extent of bare rock of granulated stone than any other.'

These words were written almost 200 years ago, soon after Cheltenham's reputation as a spa was confirmed by the visit of George III.

1 mile

Within a few years, quarrying for the building of Regency Cheltenham was to expose even more bare rock — in 1810, a ton of dressed stone from Dead Man's quarry cost one penny, delivery included. It was not until 1926 that quarrying finally ceased at Leckhampton and the hill became a public leisure area under the ownership of Cheltenham Borough Council. Well used it may be, but no exploration of the Cotswold uplands is complete without a scramble over this fascinating site.

Tramway Cottage, near the car park, was at the centre of stormy scenes during Edwardian times. The hill's new owner had fenced off the footpaths crossing his ground and had built a cottage to house his quarry foreman. The local council objected to his high-handed attitude but failed to act decisively to oppose it. Tired of waiting for their rights to be restored, a group of local working men, known as the Leckhampton Stalwarts, took the law into their own hands and after forcibly ejecting the foreman, demolished the cottage and pulled down the fences. The ringleaders were eventually arrested, tried and sent to prison, but public opinion was on their side and soon afterwards the hill was resold and the public rights of way restored.

During the last few years of their operation, the quarries were worked by a company with expansive ideas, and it is the remains of their regime — a broad-gauge rail incline and the weed-choked ruins of lime kilns that are seen on the climb through the trees to the Devil's Chimney.

This landmark, the pride of Cheltenham, was created early in the 19th century as a result of the cutting of a tramway incline high on the rock face. It became a valuable publicity feature, much drawn, painted, photographed —

and even climbed until recent years when fears of its collapse led to expensive restoration work and the banning of climbing.

While those with a liking for industrial archaeology are pottering about in search of stone sleepers and the rusting remnants of rails and winches, the geologically inclined are spoiled for choice. Fossils are hard to come by in the great blocks of freestone — so called because of the ease with which it can be quarried — but are plentiful in the ragstones which lie above them. This stone is suitable only for drystone walling and is rich in bivalve fossils, especially gryphaea — the familiar Devil's toenail — which resemble large oysters.

Botanically, Leckhampton Hill provides both unimproved limestone grassland habitat and also mixed woodland. Distinctive on the short turf are such flowers as the blue harebell, scabious, violet and milkwort, the yellow cowslip, hairy St. John's wort, yellowwort, rock rose and bird's foot trefoil, and the tiny mauve wild thyme and white eyebright.

Such a varied flora attracts many butterflies, which, together with an interesting bird population, add further appeal to the hill.

Not surprisingly, the Iron Age inhabitants of the Cotswolds left their mark on Leckhampton Hill. Above the edge of Dead Man's Quarry can be seen the remains of their 7-acre univallate hill fort,

A typical Severn foreshore scene. It show 'putts', or fish traps, secured along a wooden frame. Behind them is Sedbury Cliff, two miles upstream from the Severn Bridge. Page 127.

Offa's Dyke begins its Marches trail on top of Sedbury Cliffs high over the Severn, close by Chepstow. The commemorative stone is accessible to any fit walker wishing to experience the curiously dramatic spot. Page 128.

Nottingham Hill in the middle distance views from above one of Cleeve Commons old quarries, one-time source of the famous Cotswold stone. Page 70.

The Devil's Chimney lies beside the waymarked Cotswold Way long distance footpath immediately over Gloucester. The lower section is a natural rock formation but it was capped a century ago by local quarrymen when their quarry closed.
Page 74.

Old Father Thames guards his river's uppermost lock by Lechlade. The statue was commissioned in 1851 by the Merchants of London for the Great (Crystal Palace) Exhibition, originally as Neptune, some say. Page 108

The view along Birdlip Hill, immediately below the car park, now thankfully remote from the busy A417. Few visitors stray far from their cars so although the spot is deservedly popular the grassy slopes are usually quiet and empty. Page 78.

The intriguingly named New Fancy View, from the top of which one may gaze across the Forest of Dean, is in fact the landscaped tip, or slag-heap, of the old New Fancy Colliery. Page 28.

Looking westward along the central Broad Ride of Cirencester Park. The Park is privately owned by the Earl of Bathurst who has granted general public access. The Ride is five miles long and allows one to walk without hindrance deep into fine wooded countryside.

In the opposite direction along Broad Ride is Cirencester and its parish church, St. John the Baptist. It is doubtful that more convenient countryside access is to be found anywhere in the county. Page 100.

Shelley's Walk runs between Lechlade parish church, where Shelley composed his "Here could I hope that death did hide from human sights sweet secrets" and the statue of Old Father Thames, the excellent Trout Inn close by. Page 108.

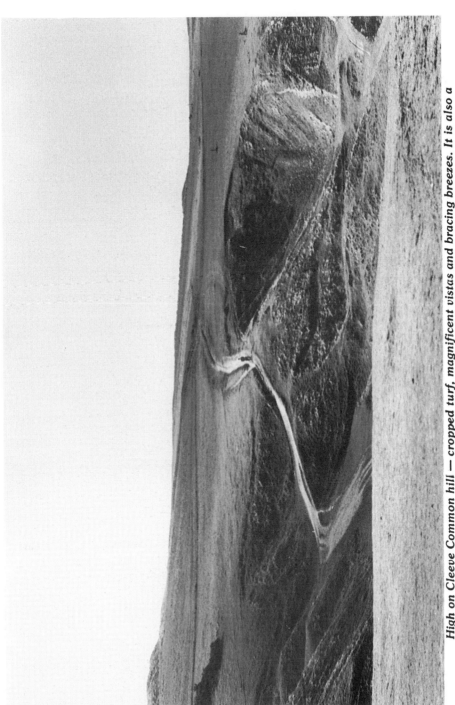

High on Cleeve Common hill — cropped turf, magnificent vistas and bracing breezes. It is also a golf course. Page 70.

The magnificently designed portal of the Thames and Severn canal tunnel at Sapperton near Coates. It was built in 1789 and only recently restored. Pages 103, 125.

Bledington village and ducks on the green. Page 64.

Wyck Rissington village green, the largest green in Gloucester and certainly one of the most beautiful. In its lovely village church Gustav Holst was organist. Page 68.

which excavation in 1970 revealed to have been destroyed by fire.

Many visitors to Leckhampton Hill come for the fresh air and the superb views, both are well worth the climb. On a clear day, the Black Mountains can be picked out, together with Clee Hill in Shropshire, while the proud Malverns are revealed in splendour. Below lies Cheltenham, part Regency elegance, part commonplace clutter of later times. It is to the best of Cheltenham's buildings that our thoughts turn however, for the stone that built them came from these long-silent quarries of Leckhampton Hill.

Charlton Kings Common

Map 163, GR 967/177. Location sketchmap see page 73.
Parking: Limited, on verge near first left-hand bend along u/c road off A 435 just N of junction with A436.

A 76-acre extension of Leckhampton Hill, offering good views and exhilarating walking along undulating stretch of Cotswold Way. Optional steep descent to lower slopes.

Charlton Kings Common is the name given to the south-eastern extremity of Leckhampton Hill and as such can be explored in conjunction with the rest of that extensive and rewarding area. However, for those wishing to confine their visit exclusively to the common, the directions given here should prove useful, despite the fact that parking close to the entrance to the lane waymarked 'Leckhampton Hill 2.5 km' is somewhat limited.

Although this lane is part of the Cotswold Way, there is no indication, as it strikes off between tall hedges of thorn, hazel and whitebeam, festooned with old man's beard, that it leads the walker towards a steep hillside offering splendid views.

Suddenly, however, the landscape away to the east is revealed, with a patchwork of small irregular fields covering the middle ground, beyond which the higher wolds sweep boldly layer upon layer towards the open sky. Soon the path climbs over the sinewy roots of ancient beeches and the golfers dotted on their pocket-handkerchief greens below are obscured spasmodically from view by clumps of gorse.

The walking is full of interest now. Blue harebells toss in the summer breeze and Roman snails, with their large creamy-brown shells — said to have been imported to supplement the invaders' diet — can be seen feeding on the low vegetation in damp conditions.

Charlton Kings — an ancient and historic village struggling to preserve its identity in the face of Cheltenham's sprawl — stretches away to the right and as the path swings left, Cheltenham itself comes into view ahead. Those deciding to continue to the Devil's Chimney on Leckhampton Hill should keep on along this path. Those wishing to return to the start by a different route can do so by swinging sharp left to follow a footpath alongside a ruinous wall to Hartley Farm, where by turning left they can walk along the minor road back to the car.

Crickley Hill Country Park

**Map 163, GR 928/163.
Parking: Official car park off B4070, close to roundabout at junction of A436 and A417.**

A 114-acre country park, jointly owned by GCC and NT, offering graded walking, superb views, geological, wildlife and above all, exceptional archaeological interest. Information centre. Toilets.

Anyone inclined to avoid all country parks as over-popular playgrounds for the masses, really should make an exception over Crickley Hill. For here, 875 feet above sea level on the Cotswold escarpment, yet within a few miles of both Gloucester and Cheltenham, is a promontory hilltop offering just about everything one could ask of an expanse of inland countryside anywhere in lowland Britain.

Until 1963, Crickley Hill's 160 million-year old beds of Middle Jurassic limestone were quarried for stone for road-making and constructional filling. Before then, this rock, being generally too coarse and friable for use as building stone, was burned in the coke-fired kilns to produce quicklime. Earlier still, the older quarries on the hill yielded stone for drystone wall-building, examples of which can be seen locally, including a recently-built section of wall at the south-western extremity of the park.

It was in 1969 that Crickley Hill first began to yield up its archaeological past to the brushes and trowels of Dr. Philip Dixon and his teams of international volunteers. Since then, every summer has seen these dedicated archaeologists return to unearth new evidence of prehistoric life on the hilltop site. So far, over a million items have been found, representing human occupation of Crickley from the Neolithic, through the late Bronze Age and into the Iron Age periods, as well as proof of early post-Roman habitation.

Altogether, two decades of excavation have revealed over twenty phases of settlement, the earliest of which was a Neolithic village containing a rectangular wooden house. Apparently, about 3,500 years ago, this was burned down by attackers armed with bows, flint-tipped arrows from which were found embedded in the timbers.

There seems to have followed a quiet period of more than a thousand years in the history of Crickley Hill, during which there were no permanent settlers. Round about 700 BC, however, new colonists constructed long rectangular buildings on a nine-acre site defended by ramparts, ditches and stone walls, which in turn was destroyed and abandoned about a century later.

The last prehistoric settlement — a village consisting of round houses — seems to have had only a short existence before destruction came, while the most recent site — a few dwellings dating from post-Roman times - was uncovered on the hill's inhospitable southern flank in 1982.

During late July and August, visitors to the country park can view the archaeological work in progress. At other times, coloured posts and information display boards indicate the locations of major structures.

As well as geology and archaeology, Crickley Hill offers considerable wildlife interest. The area known as the Scrubbs is typical beech woodland with demonstration areas of hazel coppice. The nearby grassland supports a varied ground flora, including field scabious, rock rose, wild thyme and several species of orchid, while both butterfly and bird populations are extensive. Lists of flora and fauna to watch out for, compiled by the park's warden, are displayed at the Information Centre.

Last, but by no means least, mention must be made of Crickley's views. From this fine promontory can be seen a wide sweep of the silver-coiling Severn, the Robinswood and Churchdown outlier hills, the sprawl of Gloucester, and the distant outlines of the Welsh mountains. Those for whom isolation is vital may find this, like other country parks, a little too popular at peak holiday times and at weekends. Otherwise Crickley Hill is a marvellous amenity with pleasures in plenty to suit every possible taste.

Barrow Wake, Birdlip

Map 163, GR 932/153.
Location sketchmap see page 73.
Parking: Official viewpoint car park, off Birdlip turn from A417.

26 acres of steep open grassland, reached from popular viewpoint.

Considered one of the finest viewpoints in the Cotswolds, Barrow Wake draws many motorists off the busy A417 but mercifully of the few that stir from their cars, only a minority venture beyond the two excellent topographs (one of which had succumbed to vandals at the time of this survey).

This, in other words, is more than a viewpoint. It is an extensive area of unimproved limestone grassland growing on steep irregular terrain created by the so-called slumping of shaley rocks on the underlying beds of limestone.

There are patches of oak scrub too, and clumps of larch, as well as a scatter of ash, hawthorn, whitebeam, sycamore, elder and holly, but the main natural history interest is the grassland which, together with its distinctive geology, account for its Site of Special Scientific Interest status.

This steep, sparse grassland supports a healthy population of lime-loving wild flowers. Wood sage, rock rose, sald burnet and the other characteristic species are soon found — it may call for more time and effort to locate the delicate little musk orchid with its yellowish-green flowers smelling more of honey than musk, but a search during June or July should reveal its presence.

Among the insects, two species to watch out for are the chalkhill blue and the Duke of Burgundy fritillary. Grasshoppers abound here and glow-worms have been recorded. On sunny days, adders bask motionless in the open, so cautious progress is called for.

Apart from the crows, which perform a range of aerial agilities in the wind, bird life tends to be concentrated in the scrubby margins. An exception is the handsome summer-visiting redstart, a few pairs of which nest in crevices in the old stone walls at the foot of the slopes. Although some distance below, their fiery-coloured tails are visible from the lower paths of the Wake.

It was during quarrying operations to the east of the present road, in 1879, that one of the most significant Iron Age burials in the Cotswolds was discovered. This was the grave of a woman, whose face had been covered by a large bronze bowl and at whose side had been laid a remarkable collection of grave goods. These included a silver brooch, a bronze bangle, a knife, a bowl, tweezers — and an ornate bronze mirror with decorated incised, curvilinear designs on the back while the handle was inlaid with enamel.

After having been hidden from view for over 1800 years, this "Birdlip Mirror", together with the other treasures are now in Gloucester Museum. Did its owner, we find ourselves speculating, get pleasure from this superb view? Did her eyes leave her mirror and sweep appreciatively from Robinswood Hill, via distant May Hill to the Malverns and eastward to Leckhampton and Cleeve, before resting finally on the rocky face of Crickley over the valley below?

All we can be sure of is that Gloucester has imposed itself on this fine view since then. Nondescript, even downright ugly, much of the city may be, but the noble cathedral tower. highlighted in a sudden shaft of sunlight, lends a dignity to the scene, helping to soften so much of the harshness that human progress has wrought here since the unknown lady gazed down from her lonely hilltop.

Ravensgate Hill Common

Map 163, GR 978/184. Parking: On verge near shooting school entrance at Cotswold Way crossing, on A436 about 1 mile E of A436/A435 junction.

Steep open common with wide views. Choice of gentle ridge walking or more testing descent and climb.

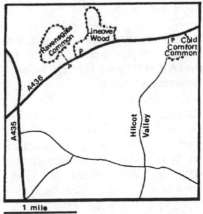

Walkers travelling the Cotswold Way from north to south have cause to remember Ravensgate Hill, for the short diagonal climb to its summit is about as steep as any faced on the entire walk.

On leaving the car, follow the Cotswold Way north across a field and through Wistley Plantation. On emerging from the woodland path via an interesting home-made gate, a memorable view awaits. Ahead lies Cheltenham with its gracious Regency buildings. Next is Charlton Kings, while the eastward-sweeping eye

79

soon settles first on Dowdeswell Reservoir and then Whittington, with its elegant Court peeping from behind the trees.

Three walking possibilities present themselves. To the right, a footpath follows the fringe of the plantation towards Lineover Wood, owned by the Woodland Trust and described elsewhere. To the left, the banks and hollows bear witness to a long-lost road which came this way before dipping down by Timbercombe

wood towards Charlton Kings. The romantic appeal of this route is enhanced by the scatter of birch, gorse and limestone-loving wild flowers.

While for the energetic, who feel that must pit themselves against this (on Cotswold standards) testing terrain, there is always the option of following the Cotswold Way down the slope towards Old Dole Farm, then savouring the climb back!

Lineover Wood

Map 163, GR 984/184. Location sketchmap see page 79. Parking: On verge of A436, about 2 miles E of junction with A435.

Woodland Trust wood on steep slope with choice of paths all entailing steep return ascents.

Lineover is an easily accessible old wood that after years of neglect is at last being managed in the interests of conservation. What do we mean by old? Well, there is a record of woodland occupying the site as long ago as the 9th century and the name, experts suggest, means a lime-tree bank. The limes — of the small-leaved variety — have long since gone, but Lineover is rich in other native hardwood species for all that, with oak, ash, sycamore, hazel, holly, field maple and

hawthorn all thriving on the deep soils of the lower north-facing slopes.

Extensive planting of larch took place some years ago and there was a real danger that Lineover would lose its character as a valuable remnant of old woodland. Its timely purchase by the Woodland Trust has saved it from this ignominious fate however, and the conifer clumps are being cleared to enable the native forest trees to prosper as formerly.

In common with other similar tracts of ancient woodland, Lineover offers a succession of interest throughout the year. Early spring sees the woodland floor carpeted with dog's mercury, followed by bluebells and lily-of-the-valley. Polypody ferns adorn the stumps of old trees which, as the year advances, play host to luxuriant clusters of toadstools.

Autumn in Lineover finds the fading canopy seething with bird activity. Nomadic bands of long-tailed tits forage industriously overhead, accompanied often by a scatter of others of their tribe. Nuthatches call boldly after their fashion and gaudy jays bound from the oaks with raucous squawks of alarm. All in all, ancient Lineover looks set to grace the Cotswold escarpment above the Chelt valley for another thousand years or more.

Cold Comfort Common

Map 163, GR 004/186. Location sketchmap see page 79.
Parking: Official car park signposted Kilkenny Viewpoint, off A436, about 3 miles E of junction with A435.

Popular viewpoint with easy, although limited, walking possibilities.

'Kilkenny Viewpoint', proclaims the signpost indicating this stretch of grassland and scrub, a short distance from the Kilkenny Inn. And while this possesses a good deal of Irish charm, it would be a pity if its original one, Cold Comfort Common, fell into disuse.

Indeed, the winds can sweep across this exposed patch of hillside with a rare vigour at times, but for those who decide to brave the elements, these old quarry workings offer a wide scenic panorama, as well as an easy stroll over limestone grassland. This is rich in such flowers as rock rose, field scabious, wild thyme and a scatter of the commoner orchids, followed later in the year by autumn felwort — an attractive member of the gentian family.

On sunny summer days, the picnic tables prove popular and children can enjoy playing in a spacious, yet safe, environment. Such days bring out the butterflies, a speciality being the diminutive small blue.

Those wishing to stretch their legs by venturing further afield should find a leisurely amble along the minor road to Hilcot rewarding. A short distance up the slope on the left is a pine-covered mound marked as St. Paul's Epistle on maps but known locally as Bull's Pissel. It is in fact a round barrow, a prehistoric burial mound, and its official name came about because at the time of the beating of the bounds of the village of Dowdeswell, readings from that book of the Bible were given at this spot.

Buckholt Wood (incorporating Cranham Wood)

Map 163, GR 894/131.
Parking: Cranham village, off
A46, N of Painswick.

Large GTNC-managed
National Nature Reserve
intersected by public
footpaths. Some gradients
with possible difficult
stretches after rain and at
peak of summer growth.

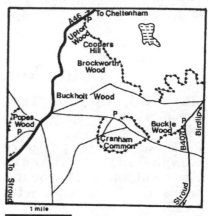

250 acres in extent, Buckholt Wood forms the largest part of a tract of country known as the Cotswold Commons and Beechwoods SSSI, and as such is one of the most important areas of wildlife habitat in the entire county. It lies to the north of the village of Cranham, from where there are several other approaches in addition to the one indicated by the grid reference above.

'The wood is all common land with access on foot throughout', states the official NNR notice. Woodland commons are a rare feature in Gloucestershire today, and the fact that Buckholt — Anglo-Saxon for beechwood — is mentioned in the Domesday Book and has been common land for 700 years, enhances its value even further as living evidence of centuries of rural development.

A brief summary of Buckholt's

long history may be of interest. Like other wooded commons, it served in prehistoric times both for grazing and timber production. This dual purpose survived into the Saxon and Norman periods, in contrast to many other similar areas, which were enclosed and cleared for agriculture.

Inevitably, there was conflict between grazing and the growing of trees for timber, and there is a record of a woodward being appointed to attend to these and other matters in 1269. Traditionally, Buckholt was managed by coppicing, which involved the cutting of underwood on a 20-year rotation, for use in charcoal-making, and for a range of crafts, as well as for firewood.

The commoners, meanwhile, exercised their rights of pannage and estover, which were practised

82

until the 17th century. As Buckholt was a beechwood, the pannage was chiefly beechmast, which in good years supported large herds of tame swine, but was an unreliable source of food generally.

Estover was the name for the right to collect dead wood and windblown timber for firewood, not to be confused with certain other rights applying to timber for house-building, trades, and so on.

During the 18th century, the woodland economy was in a state of flux. For some years, quantities of the best beech wood had been cut and sold to be made into gun stocks in Birmingham, but by the mid-19th century, both this requirement and the long-standing demand for charcoal had declined, and so Buckholt was sold.

The end of the charcoal-making-era saw a change from coppice to high-forest timber production. It is still possible to pick out some of the old beech coppice stools, as well as a few pollards — trees cut at varying heights from the ground — but the present regime of selective thinning, coupled with replanting and natural regeneration, favours wild life as well as being economically viable.

So although commoners still hold their traditional rights to graze sheep, cattle and horses in Buckholt Wood, this superb unenclosed beechwood is best known as an invaluable wildlife habitat, supporting a rich flora, rare bats and molluscs, and good bird and butterfly populations.

Cooper's Hill
(including Upton & Brockworth Woods)

Maps 162 and 163, GR 886/140. Location sketchmap see page 82.
Parking: Official car park, off A46, 1 mile SW of junction with A417.

Extensive tract of beech woodland with network of public paths, some steep. Muddy patches after rain. Car park toilets.

Although its name suggests a link with barrels, it is for rolling out cheeses seven pound Double Gloucester ones, of course — that Cooper's Hill is renowned. Here, on this hilltop on Spring Bank Holiday Monday, crowds gather to watch local daredevils compete in chasing these down the one-in-one slope, risking life and limb for the prize of a mere cheese. In these modern times, they are safe in the knowledge that a fleet of ambulances is ready and waiting at the foot of the slope in case the worst happens.

The cheese-rolling ceremony was formerly held on Midsummer's

Day and its pagan origins are derived supposedly from a race to catch the sun and so arrest the shortening days. Another theory is that the custom originated from the re-enactment of the winning of a prehistoric battle, during which the enemy were routed by having stones rolled down on them from the hilltop.

The maypole, topped by a weathercock, perched near the summit of the slope, reminds us that other festivities also took place here in former times. As late as the Victorian era, these included wrestling, racing, face-pulling — and a chattering competition for old women with a prize of a bladder of snuff!

For those who wish to explore Cooper's Hill at quieter times, leave the car in the car park at Fiddler's Elbow and climb into Upton Wood. Soon, on the left, is a viewpoint, complete with a pictorial representation of local landmarks. The route swings and climbs to the right, following a nature trail, indicated by white posts with coloured tops. This leads the way through the beech trees of Brockworth Wood, which were coppiced for centuries by local charcoal-burners to produce fuel for iron-smelting.

The modern management cycle operated in these woods — felling and coppicing is clearly evident today, as is the mixed nature of the woodland, which in addition to beech includes ash, sycamore, field maple and holly.

The terrain between the woods of Cooper's Hill and the vast expanse of Buckholt Wood is occupied by High Brotheridge, so called from its appearance a high, broad ridge — rising to 927 feet above sea level. Prehistoric man clearly favoured this hilltop, for the remains of the rampart of a settlement, possibly of Iron Age origin, lie along its southern extremity.

Buckle Wood

Map 163, GR 915/130. Location sketchmap, see page 82. Parking: Layby off B4070, Birdlip — Stroud road, between Painswick and Cranham turns.

Part of the Cotswold Commons and Beechwoods NNR, this wood offers clear paths as well as a Neolithic long barrow which can be difficult to locate in lush summer growth.

For those who like their archaeology liberally spiced with a pinch of romance and mystery, Buckle Wood is as near perfection as can be wished for.

Here in the heart of a Cotswold beechwood lies what remains of

West Tump, a 150 feet-long and 26 feet-wide Neolithic long barrow which had remained undisturbed for close on 4000 years until it was accidentally discovered by the indefatigable antiquary George Witts, in 1880. Witts wasted no time in obtaining permission to excavate his find.

Like Belas Knap, West Tump had a false entrance between two 'horns' and a burial chamber roughly half way along the mound. In this, twenty skeletons were found and four more in the nearby forecourt, while at the far end of the chamber was discovered a semi-circular platform on which were the crouched remains of a young woman and an infant.

West Tump may have yielded up its secrets but it still exerts a hold over the curious. Locating it is a challenge in itself. You need to strike off to the right of the main woodland ride, picking your way along narrow, branching paths and negotiating bramble trip-wires to the highest part of the wood in the hope of spotting the tree-topped mound through the foliage.

Sadly, the barrow's condition a century after its excavation is far removed from the 'very perfect' state in which George Witts discovered it. Overgrown, riddled with rabbit burrows and hemmed in by trees, it seems in danger of crumbling away for ever.

Is finding it worth the effort? The answer depends on whether or not you are responsive to the pull of the ancient past. If, on the other hand, your idea of happiness is to savour dappled sunlight filtering through the beech canopy, or to linger amidst patches of bluebells, woodruff or sanicle, or perhaps merely to lean on a beech trunk and listen to the quivering trill of the wood warbler, then Buckle Wood needs no elusive archaeological relic to draw you — it has all you desire already, and more besides.

Pope's Wood

Map 162, GR 876/127. Location sketchmap see page 82.
Parking: By woodland edge at top of lane from A46 alongside Royal William Inn, 3 miles N Painswick.

A 64-acre ancient beechwood, managed by GTNC and crossed by tracks and paths, from which visitors should not stray.

The western extremity of the Cotswold Commons and Beechwoods NNR, Pope's Wood commands the limestone scarp between Prinknash Park and Painswick Beacon. Footpaths radiate out towards Prinknash, Upton St. Leonards, Cud Hill and Spoonbed Hill, while other routes lead over the golf links and on to Painswick Beacon.

Once managed as coppiced woodland, Pope's Wood now comprises mature stands of beech, with ash, whitebeam, wayfaring tree and hazel also prominent.

Fortunately, the need to keep strictly to the paths in no way inhibits the naturalist. In spring, before the beech canopy closes over, dog violets, wood anemones and bluebells provide charm and colour in generous measure, while during late summer, the clumps of hemp agrimony in the clearings serve to lure the handsome silver-washed fritillary butterfly, a strong flyer which can be approached with stealth and studied at close quarters.

Pope's Wood also provides ideal breeding habitat for the wood warbler, whose persistent accelerating trill is a feature during May and June. Of the resident bird species, the marsh tit, a dapper little bird with a distinctive scolding note, the loud-whistling nuthatch, and the upward spiralling mouse-like treecreeper, are all in evidence during the spring and early summer.

Cranham Common

Map 163, GR 895/126. Location sketchmap see page 82. Parking: Cranham village, off A46, N of Painswick.

Open grassy common crossed by unfenced roads linking two parts of village. Steep wooded southern fringe.

This is about as near to the conventional image of a common as can be found in the Cotswolds. Yet to most people, the name Cranham is synonymous with beech woodlands in the Cotswolds. Cranham Woods, described in this book under the heading of Buckholt Wood, are rightly extolled as one of the glories of the region.

A glance at the map reveals that woodland still hems in Cranham to the north and east, with other tracts away to the south and west. This makes the origin of the name — place of the cranes — appear somewhat odd, attributable perhaps to the presence of herons by the Painswick stream, along which these ponderous yet wily birds still occasionally beat their way.

Cranham's big day is the second Monday in August, when crowds gather for the Feast, held in honour of St. James the Great, Patron Saint of the village church. A boundary race commemorates the traditional beating of the bounds, a tug-o'-war is a symbolic reminder of long-forgotten strife with neighbouring villages, and a deer is roasted and a mime performed of the giving of venison by the squire to the villagers.

Cranham has long lost its pottery, its corn mill and its charcoal-burning industry but the good news is that traditional Cotswold sheep still graze on its common. These were reintroduced by a common-management group a few years ago in an attempt to maintain the open grassland in the time-honoured manner. To counter difficulties over straying, experiments have been carried out by the Royal Agricultural College, Cirencester, with collars containing electronic gadgets, which bleep when the wearers get too close to cables laid on the ground around the perimeter of their grazing area.

Thanks to the sheep, the scrub which threatened to banish the lime-loving flowers from Cranham Common is now being kept in check. Wander from the village towards the church and the school and you will enjoy enchanting views away to the beeches of Buckholt Woods. But if planning a winter visit, be warned! The winds sweep across the open common with a rare vigour; little wonder that while staying here, the composer Gustav Holst took the poem 'In the Bleak Midwinter', and set it to music, calling it Cranham. One fancies he must have tramped the exposed common road at a time when winter was at its worst to have captured the sombre mood to such perfection.

Painswick Beacon ⊕

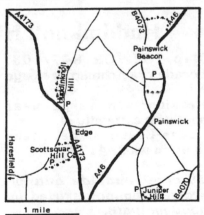

1 mile

**Map 162, GR 868/118.
Parking: Ample along u/c road crossing Beacon and linking A46 and B4073.**

Easily accessible 166-acre upland tract, well loved by golfers, picnickers — and the rest of the world!

Rising to 931 feet above sea level, Painswick Beacon (Painswick Hill on maps) has long been an attraction to visitors and such popularity has exacted its price. Nothing can detract from the marvellous views of course, but seething humanity, its cars, and above all, its litter, are an inescapable part of the modern scene throughout the summer months, not to mention the hazard of golf balls, so be prepared!

Iron Age people laboured to fortify this hilltop, and we can still see — and wonder at — their endeavours. They built a fort with a double rampart and these, together with banks and ditches, made a virtually impregnable defensive position.

Centuries of quarrying have reduced this fortress to its present sorry state, and people-pressure continues to wear away at their ancient handiwork. The inexorable spread of seeding Scots pines further reduces the impact of the earthwork, while at the same time posing a growing threat to the hill's limestone grassland flora, once highly acclaimed by botanists.

For many walkers, Painswick Beacon is part of the Cotswold Way experience, for this long-distance footpath traverses the hill on its way from Pope's Wood to Painswick. There are other tempt-

ing paths and crooked lanes too, including one dipping to the east of the A46 to a sheltered little combe called Paradise, a name attributed to none other than Charles I, who came to know the locality well when staying at Painswick during the siege of Gloucester in 1643.

Alas for the king and his cause, his last memories of the Beacon were far from happy ones. After the Royalist forces had withdrawn from their siege positions at the approach of a Parliamentary army from London, the tired and dispirited soldiers spent a night camped in the ditches of the old fort. Legend has it that on asking his father, the King, if they could now go home, the boy Prince of Wales received the answer 'My son, we have no home.'

Huddinknoll Hill Common, Edge

Map 162, GR 847/103. Location sketchmap see page 87. Parking: On verge near southerly extremity of Seven-Leaze Lane, near junction with A4173.

10-acre roadside quarry-scarred common skirted by good footpath.

A curving ridge-like hill with a longer-than-usual name to match, Huddinknoll stands at over 600 feet above the Vale of Gloucester, two miles north-west of Painswick.

A footpath extends along its complete length, giving a pleasant walk between woodland and old quarries. This can be followed from the start of Seven-Leaze Lane, which leaves the A4173 to the north of Edge church, with the options of retracing steps or strolling back along the lane fringing the common.

Gaps in the trees enable excellent views to be had south-westwards of the wooded escarpment through which the Cotswold Way passes on its approach to Haresfield Beacon. Further westwards, beyond a landscape of crumpled fields scattered with farmsteads, the Severn glistens in the sunshine as it sweeps in a great loop round the Arlingham peninsula.

Less dramatic, though pleasing enough, are the eastward views, over the little valley of the Wash Brook to Spoonbed Hill and Painswick Beacon. Those so minded, can follow a footpath over part of this pastoral scene which crosses a wall over a stile opposite the northern extremity of the common.

Twice in history, the peace of Huddinknoll Hill has been violated by the sounds of war. In 1471, the Yorkist army of Edward IV is said to have camped here on its way to do battle with the Lancastrians at Tewkesbury. But it was in the second of the country's terrible internecine conflicts, the Civil War, that Huddinknoll Hill witnessed the true horror of combat. On a wintry day in February 1644, a Roundhead force, advancing on Painswick from Gloucester, was overwhelmed by the Royalist army as it reached the hilltop. Eighty men were killed in the struggle, and local folklore has it that several of their skeletons were dug up during the last century, as well as armour and helmets, the latter being used as coal-scuttles!

The quarry-scarred face of Huddinknoll is hidden in summer by phalanx upon phalanx of rosebay willowherb, a glorious sight. Less welcome is the more recent arrival of a thicket of Japanese knotweed, a persistent colonist in such wild places as this, and, unlike the willowherb, adding little by way of colour to a peaceful spot where strife is but a fading memory.

Scottsquar Hill Common, Edge

Map 162, GRs 850/091 and 847/093. Location sketchmap see page 87. Parking: Reached along A4173, Gloucester — Pitchcombe — Stroud road. Best access along Cotswold Way opposite Edgemoor Inn, but parking for non-customers difficult. Alternative parking: Old quarries along u/c Edge — Haresfield road, half-a-mile SW Edge church.

A steeply-sloping 55-acre grassland common, with scattered trees and old quarries. Sweeping views over Painswick valley

Few hostelries can offer better views than the Edgemoor Inn, known as the Gloucester House in coaching days, when this road was the main thoroughfare to Stroud. From opposite the inn, the Cotswold Way long-distance-footpath climbs the lower slopes of the common. Here, colonisation by birch, though a fine, graceful tree in its rightful place, is beginning to have a detrimental effect on the limestone flora.

The range of flowers, in common with other limestone-grassland localities in the vicinity, is extremely varied. As many as six species of orchid have been recorded, although the absence of grazing in recent years has enabled coarse grasses to thrive. On sunny summer days, the climb is enriched by the presence of a range of butterflies, including the marbled white, small and common blue, and large and small skipper.

Quarrying of the Lower Inferior Oolite no longer takes place and the quarries at the top of the common are rapidly being colonised by plants. Sadly, fly-tippers and litter louts defile this part of Scottsquar.

The association of the hill's name with the northern race is purely coincidental, being derived from the Old English 'sceot' meaning steep, and 'quar', the local abbreviation for a quarry.

Juniper Hill, Painswick

Map 162, GR 866/083. Location sketchmap see page 87.
Parking: On verge at junction of Stepping Stone Lane and Yokehouse Lane, 1 mile S of Painswick.

25 acres of steeply sloping grassland littered with old quarries and scrub. Going difficult away from one clearly defined path.

The countryside around the little town of Painswick consists of a delightful switchback of rolling hills and sheltered north-east to south-west valleys, with rushing streams that once powered the cloth mills that brought prosperity to the region.

A network of winding lanes follow these valleys, all ancient ways, all bearing distinctive names. From

the junction of two of these— Stepping Stone Lane and Yokehouse Lane — a stoney track climbs by old quarries up Juniper Hill. Below, to the right, stretches Wick Street, the old road that once linked Painswick and Stroud, while hidden from view over the wide rim of the hilltop, lies Slad, clinging to the flank of its own writhing valley, the village that, through the pen of native author Laurie Lee, will always be associated with 'Cider with Rosie'.

Juniper Hill (not to be confused with another hill of the same name near Edgeworth) is in some ways typical of the extensive areas of limestone grassland, pockmarked with old quarries, that are a feature of the central Cotswolds. Unimproved agriculturally, and not subjected to regular grazing by livestock, these areas must at an earlier stage have supported outstandingly varied wild flower populations. Unfortunately however, the absence of grazing allows scrub to invade, which eventually covers the ground and, in time, produces woodland.

As the name suggests, Juniper Hill once had a thriving colony of this distinctive evergreen shrub but, as on other local sites, juniper is a declining species and only a few old and decrepit bushes now survive.

The scrub meanwhile, tightens its hold. Without exception, attractive in their own right, the spreading yews, birches, oaks and whitebeams are a lethal combination as far as ground flora is concerned, which in turn, means that, unless the scrub's advance is checked, grassland butterflies too, will diminish as their habitat shrinks.

Having lamented the spread of scrub on Cotswold grassland, it may be worth considering here the attributes of this habitat. These can be summarised as providing nesting sites for birds — several species of tits and warblers breed in scrub — and in supporting populations of certain species of butterflies, notably the ringlet, hedge brown and green hairstreak.

While for those for whom mistletoe is usually seen only in inaccessible treetops, this unique yellow-green parasite has established itself on whitebeam saplings across Juniper Hill and can therefore be studied at close quarters.

Juniper shrub

Sheepscombe Common

Map 163, GR 892/104.
Parking: Sheepscombe village, off A46 between Painswick and Cranham Corner. Common reached on foot up lane to left of inn, opposite Old Vicarage.

A 12-acre common perched high on rough ground. Outstanding views and wildlife interest.

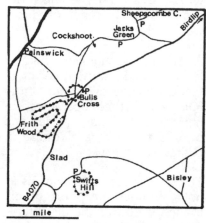

Sheepscombe is one of the remotest villages in the Cotswolds, tucked away down narrow twisting lanes that not only make a sensitive motorist feel an intruder, but demand driving skills — and patience — of the highest order. Even after finding the place, there remains the problem of parking, for Sheepscombe folk, far from pandering to visitors, seem to do their level best to discourage them. Even the Ordnance Survey appear to have a hand in this conspiracy: Sheepscombe lies at the very edge of the sheet.

Superb views reward the walker after the stiff climb to reach this common, which lies to the north of the village and commands the valley. To the south stands the tiny turret of the early 19th century church, while away to the west rises 'Painswick Proud', elegant in its pale grey stone from here as from every other direction.

This was an open common once, regularly grazed and supporting as rich a population of lime-loving flowers as one could wish for. In the absence of grazing, an attempt is made to control the spread of scrub — oak, birch and whitebeam, chiefly — but the struggle is an uphill one. Even so, mounds, hollows and exposures of outcropping white limestone still provide congenial conditions for a scatter of characteristic flowers, of which horseshoe vetch is, in particular, prominent. In May and June, grasshoppers add their own distinctive music to the exhuberant outpourings of the tree pipits, while the air is full of butterflies dancing over the flower-spangled turf. At such times, the big, wide, outside world seems a mere irrelevance.

Jack's Green & Cockshoot Commons, Sheepscombe ⊕

Map 162, GRs Jacks Green 888/099, Cockshoot 882/098
Location sketchmap see page 92.
Parking: Tucked well into verge by Jacks Green, on u/c Sheepscombe — B4070 road, 2 miles E Painswick.

Two small grassy commons linked by public path along woodland fringe.

These two small commons are in the heart of 'Cider with Rosie' country, south of the village of Sheepscombe. Linked by a public footpath along the edge of Blackstable Wood, they offer superb views northwards beyond the village roofs and over the valley of the Painswick stream to Saltridge Hill woods.

Parking is limited along the road by Jacks Green. Leave the car tucked in as tightly as possible and after admiring the view, climb the track to the right to follow the path for a half-mile or so inside the woodland edge to Cockshoot. Here, scrub-encroachment has reached an advanced stage and clumps of silver birch are well established.

From Cockshoot's slope, the graceful little town of Painswick can be seen away to the west. Termed 'Painswick Proud' in an old rhyme, this is one of the few towns that manages to look alluring from whatever viewpoint it is gazed upon. Much visited on account of its 'wool' tombs, its 99 churchyard yews and its annual 'clipping' ceremony, the scars it sustained from bomb damage in the second World War have long since healed.

Bird lovers lingering by Blackstable Wood in spring may well hear the tree pipit's tireless, bold refrain as he 'parachutes' down to his chosen perch. Others may opt for settling down on the hillside for a final feasting on the view, or perhaps to re-read a favourite chapter of 'Cider with Rosie'.

Tree pipit

Bulls Cross & Frith Wood

**Map 162, 877/087. Location sketchmap see page 92.
Parking: On verge of B4070, 1 mile N of Slad.**

A small common at a meeting of roads, with an adjacent 58-acre GTNC beech wood.

A lonely cross-roads despite being astride the B4070 from Slad to Birdlip, Bulls Cross, with its old milestone and wedges of open common, exerts a strong pull on the curious-minded.

Locals will tell you that the place has a sinister reputation, with stories of the bleached bones of highwaymen swinging from gibbets, and other dark doings a'plenty in distant times.

Such tales may or may not add to the appeal of Bulls Cross today. For many who linger here, the views of Painswick and the line of the woods will be sufficient in themselves, and there are few woods more alluring than Frith wood, intersected by tracks and public footpaths, including the right of way from adjacent Bull's Cross.

The name frith, an Early English word for a wooded area, suggests that there has been woodland here for hundreds of years. However, the magnificent beeches we

see today were not planted until the beginning of the 19th century. They are cared for today by a management policy entailing the selective thinning of some mature specimens to allow regeneration to take place, hopefully in time, producing a 'natural' beechwood. This will consist of trees of differing ages, together with a shrub layer of yew, holly, field maple and whitebeam.

Frith Wood stands high on the ridge between the Painswick and Slad valleys, and the beeches, although the most successful trees on the shallow brashy Cotswold soils, have suffered badly in the severe gales of recent years. The richer soils of the south-eastern extremities of the wood favour such deeper-rooted trees as the pedunculate oak, ash and sycamore. The latter though, is a rapid coloniser and is therefore kept under strict control, either by means of felling or by ring-barking, which results in dead wood, providing rich potential for excavating birds such as nuthatches and woodpeckers.

Those following the bridleway along the northern edge of the wood can walk a circular route by continuing beyond over a field to reach a track, turning left along it and returning to Bulls Cross along the footpath inside the wood's southern boundary.

Swift's Hill

Map 162, GR 876/067.
Location sketchmap see page
92.
Parking: Limited along u/c
road signposted Elcombe, off
B4070, half-a-mile S of Slad.

25 acres of steep limestone-grassland common. Owned by GTNC, but unfenced and with public access.

In the same way that 'Cider with Rosie' evokes the spirit of the Slad Valley of old in human terms, Swift's Hill is a precious remnant of the flora-rich grasslands that covered much of the region until comparatively recent times.

Designated as an SSSI in 1966, and purchased by the GTNC in the following year, Swift's Hill has survived the scourge of agricultural improvement partly because of its common-land status and partly because its steepness rendered it unsuitable for cultivation. Unfortunately, because an unfenced road runs along its foot, graziers have for a few years been reluctant to use the land as several animals have been killed by thoughtless motorists who speed along the narrow road quite unsuited to fast traffic. This undergrazing has resulted in an intrusive spread of two coarse colonisers, tor grass and upright brome, whose presence has a detrimental effect on the flora. However, since 1989, this has been countered to some extent by selective cattle grazing.

Why is it that such a bleak, sparsely-grassed upland expanse as Swift's Hill is so botanically rich? To borrow the comedian's catchphrase: 'The answer lies in the soil' — in this case, well-drained rendzinas which, though thin, provide ideal habitat for an extensive range of lime-loving, flowering plants, of which the orchids are especially well represented.

Throughout spring and summer, therefore, Swift's Hill is one of the most rewarding sites for the botanist. Take a picnic or a good identification book, and above all, take your time. Linger long on this steep hillside, enjoying not only the dazzling display of wild flowers but the butterflies too. Watch carefully and you will also observe two day-flying moths, both with dark velvet-green wings and red spots. These are the cinnabar and six-spot burnet. There are grasshoppers, too, while among the rubble in the nearby abandoned quarry can be found, as well as yet more flowers, both the slow worm and the common lizard, basking among the fossil-rich ragstones that are the delight of geologists.

Haresfield Beacon

**Map 162, GR 820/088.
Parking: On verge of u/c
Edge — Haresfield road, 3
miles NW Stroud.**

*Well known NT-owned
archaeological site and
viewpoint. Easy walking.*

"A quite unique vantage point, superior to any other on Cotswold
for the hardly credible distances
the eye can range." So wrote
H.J. Massingham, some sixty
years ago.

On a clear day, it is easy to understand Massingham's enthusiasm.
For the Beacon, which is as dramatic a spot as any south of the
Malverns, and the views it offers,
are equally impressive.

This is all the more surprising
considering the easy approach.
For it is but a short walk from the
road alongside the 1:4 sign,
through stiles and along the well-trodden Cotswold Way over Ring
Hill, to reach the triangulation pillar at 713 feet above sea level.
Quarrying has destroyed much of
early man's handiwork — a hill
fort of about four acres enclosed
by a single rampart — but it is the
views that bring us here and we
cannot fail to echo Massingham's
praise.

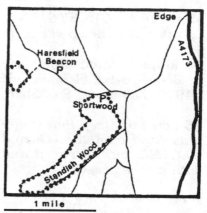

1 mile

Ranging from the patchwork of
the Vale of Berkeley to the Severn's spectacular sweep around
the Arlingham peninsula backed
by the Forest of Dean, the near
and middle distance present a
memorable picture. Beyond into
the heart of Wales, the Sugar
Loaf dominates, while away into
Shropshire, the Clee Hills rise up
beyond the Malverns. There are
glimpses on the clearest of days
of the Mendips and beyond in
Bridgewater Bay, of the Isle of
Steep Holm.

Surprisingly, Haresfield, the village which gives its name to this
splendid promontory, is a place of
the Vale. It nestles amid winding,
leafy lanes far below to the northwest, uncomfortably close to the
railway that resembles a child's
toy when viewed from the Beacon's lofty perch.

Shortwood & Standish Wood ⊕

**Map 162, GR 832/086.
Location sketchmap see page 96.
Parking: Official car park along u/c Edge — Haresfield road.**

Two contrasting, adjacent NT sites — open common and woodland. Varied walking. Good views from Shortwood. Some steep gradients in Standish Wood.

Not, as it may sound, two woods for the price of one! For although Standish Wood is true to its name, Shortwood is an adjacent wedge of Cotswold grassland notable for its sweeping views. Park in the spacious National Trust car park at Cripplegate and wander down the slope. The excellent three-dimensional topograph provides enlightenment to a growing number of visitors with every passing year.

After savouring the views return to the car park and squeeze through the wall gap on the right to reach the track into Standish Wood.

This wood, once the property of Gloucester Abbey, is an interesting mixture of plantings from several different periods. Beech is the predominant hardwood and although usually allowed to grow to its full size, there are remnants of beech coppice in the lower part of the wood and a few ancient pollarded beeches on the western boundary. Scots pine and larch plantations feature at intervals. Other trees worth searching for are aspen — a native poplar less frequently found in the Cotswolds than further north — whitebeam, and ash, with spindle, hawthorn, field maple, holly and wild privet conspicuous in the understorey.

The ground flora consists of dog's mercury, bluebell, wood anemone, yellow archangel, wood spurge and two much more unusual plants, the saprophytic bird's nest orchid and the similarly named, although unrelated, yellow bird's nest.

Among the butterflies, both the pearl-bordered and silver-washed fritillaries frequent the wood.

For a pleasant two-mile woodland ramble, follow the Cotswold Way signs (yellow arrows and white dots). In a mile, just beyond a stile, take a right-hand path which eventually dips steeply down to join a bridleway. Turn right along it and climb, keeping left at a fork, and right at a second back up to the car park.

Chedworth Woods

Map 163. GR 053/134.
Parking: Roman Villa car park (National Trust). Reached by following signs from A 429 between Northleach and Fossebridge.

Extensive private woodland intersected by public footpaths connecting Roman villa and Chedworth village. Some steep and muddy stretches.

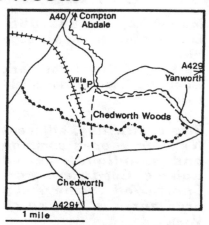

Indirectly, Chedworth Woods are among the best-known in the Cotswolds, for they form a beautiful backdrop for the Roman villa, one of the area's finest attractions.

Steps on the left before the bridge climb to the GTNC's linear nature reserve. This is a mile of the track-bed, cutting and embankment of the former Cheltenham — Cirencester railway line, which closed in 1961 and was purchased by the GTNC eight years later. It is of special interest to geologists, for its cuttings reveal good exposures of oolitic limestone of the Middle Jurassic period (180 million years ago). The exposures are rich in bivalve and brachiopod fossils and visitors are allowed to search for these in the scree. Please do not damage the rock faces — and beware of basking adders!

Chedworth Woods, stretching for over two miles along the southern bank of the River Coln, comprise the second-largest tract of woodland in the entire Cotswolds. The public paths are few but clearly defined, and from them it is possible to obtain a good idea of the structure of this semi-natural woodland, chiefly of ash and pedunculate oak, which also contains large areas of hazel coppice.

Few Gloucestershire woods are more likely to provide sightings of deer than these. Altogether three species are present — fallow, roe and the small imported muntjac — but it is the handsome fallow, conspicuous by the prominent dark line down the centre of the back and the whitish blotches on the sides during the summer months, that is likely to be glimpsed from the woodland paths.

Siccaridge, Frampton & Sapperton Woods

Map 163, GR 936/035.
Parking: Limited roadside parking along u/c Sapperton — Tunley and Waterlane road.

A group of interesting woods, rich in wildlife, with footpath access. Some steep gradients and muddy stretches in wet weather.

1 mile

There are three splendid tracts of woodland in the Frome valley, with Siccaridge (68 acres) separated from the other two by the tiny river, and also by the Thames-Severn canal. This section of the waterway, like Siccaridge Wood, is leased from the Bathurst Estate by the Gloucestershire Trust for Nature Conservation (see Severn — Thames Canal, page 124)

The grid reference given above relates to the stile and gate at the entrance to Siccaridge Wood, a short distance from the Tunley and Waterlane road.

Although for convenience sake, the woods are grouped together, they are managed in entirely different ways. Since its leasing to the GTNC in 1986, Siccaridge Wood has undergone a transformation. Conifers planted by the previous lessees, the Forestry Commission, are gradually being removed and the natural vegetation of ash and pedunculate oak is being thinned to promote areas of high forest. Meanwhile, in the case of the wood's extensive hazel coppice, two management methods are being used. One involves short-term rotational cutting to encourage the ground flora, the other being a longer-term cycle to promote conditions favourable to the dormouse.

Dormice, though engaging creatures, are seldom seen. They are not only secretive by habit but are at their most active at night. Old hazel coppice is a favourable habitat as the animal can hide its nests in the basal tangle of vegetation. These nests are of three different kinds — a breeding chamber, summer living quarters and - most carefully concealed of all - a hibernation nest in which the dormouse spends the winter months curled into a tight ball, wrapped inside its furry tail.

But if the dormouse itself is hard to find, the same cannot be said of the empty hazel-nut shells it leaves behind. These can be identified by the oval-shaped hole in the shell, with a smooth surface and oblique toothmarks around its perimeter.

Siccaridge Wood is also noted for its thriving colony of lily-of-the-valley, while the recent opening up of rides, pathways and clearings is already paying dividends with an improved ground cover of lime-loving plants and their associated butterfly populations.

Frampton and Sapperton Woods, by contrast, offer restricted access along public footpaths only. Impenetrable blackthorn thickets oc-cupy much of the valley floor, their dark and spiny branches encrusted with lichens. Higher up the flank of the valley, ferns — hartstongue and male fern — thrive in the half light created by the dense canopy of old oaks and beeches.

The unwary can be startled by the sudden eruption of a train from the mouth of a mile-and-a-half long tunnel which passes beneath Frampton Wood, carrying the Swindon — Stroud line.

For the dedicated walker, these three woods provide an absorbing half-day, full of contrasts. The less ambitious — and those who prefer their woods well endowed with paths and open spaces — are advised to content themselves with a ramble through Siccaridge, returning to Daneway along the canal towpath.

Cirencester Park

Map 163.

3000 acres of private parkland to which the public are admitted. Access is restricted to walkers and specifically excludes dogs.

A casual glance at the Ordnance Survey map shows an extensive area of woodland to the west of Cirencester. This sea of green, dwarfing all other dabs and streaks of colour for miles around, is Cirencester Park, 3000 acres of man-made landscape, created between the years 1704 and 1775 by Allen, the first Earl Bathurst.

A closer look at the map reveals that the Park stretches westwards from within Cirencester itself, having a central avenue, Broad Ride, extending for about five unswerving miles as far as the minor road linking Sapperton with Frampton Mansell.
The sheer vastness of Cirencester Park is difficult to appreciate from

any one access point. Gaining an idea of its size from the main entrance near the mansion itself on Cecily Hill, Cirencester, as many visitors imagine they do, is impossible.

Fortunately however, the Bathurst Estate permits walkers to explore Cirencester Park from several other access points, all of which are indicated by blue notices, which outline certain basic restrictions, including one forbidding dogs. This freedom to roam is invaluable, as it enables well-shod visitors to enjoy an absorbing day's woodland walking, and discover some of the park's intriguing mixture of follies and other architectural adornments.

Where to begin? Obviously, a first impression can be gained by starting at Cecily Hill, where the Bathurst mansion, which was built 1714-1718, is screened from the town by a magnificent yew hedge.

The house itself is not open.

Others may wish to see the polo ground, long famous as the scene for displays of royal sporting prowess. This is best approached by a drive indicated from the A419 Stroud road, 2.5 miles from Cirencester. The games are played on Sundays between May and September.

But it is to the woods west of the actual parkland that those wishing to explore this area of the Cotswolds are drawn. These consist of three distinct tracts of woodland — Overley Wood, Oakley Wood and Hailey Wood — parts of all of which most likely pre-date the Park itself and were incorporated into it by the imaginative Earl, who took a particular interest in forestry. These woods, which gave him such pleasure during a long and creative life, deserve to be considered individually.

Cotswold stone stile

Overley Wood

Map 163, GR 970/044.
Parking: Roadside verge on
u/c Daglingworth —
Sapperton road.

This is the most northerly extent of Cirencester Park, occupying almost all of the land enclosed by the triangle formed by three unclassified roads linking Daglingworth, the Duntisbournes, Edgeworth and Park Corner, Sapperton. Although access is possible via the public bridleway from Gloucester Lodge to Duntisbourne Rouse, which marks the wood's northern extremity, the best approach is from Overley Road, Daglingworth, along Overley Ride. This wide ride extends spine-like NNE through the centre of the wood, with a network of cross-rides branching off at intervals. For those who enjoy a leisurely ramble well away from the crowds, and with plenty of bird-watching and deer-spotting potential, this wood is a good prospect.

Oakley Wood

Map 163, GR 970/044.
Location sketchmap see
above.
Parking: As for Overley
Wood.

The biggest and central of the Cirencester Park woods, Oakley Wood is a splendid expanse of mixed woodland, criss-crossed by rides, drives and paths. Along these can be seen a truly amazing collection of romantic buildings erected by the Earl Bathurst to create the maximum scenic effect, while at the same time preserving what the Earl's friend, the poet Alexander Pope, described as 'The amiable simplicity of unadorned nature'.

Natural simplicity there may be, but there is also revealed a practical demonstration of geometry on a grand scale, with Broad Ride sweeping majestically through the wood. At Ten Rides, reached in just over a mile along Overley

Ride from the road of the same name, it is possible to stand at the crossing place of these two rides, with six others, all suitably named, striking off with unerring precision like spokes from a wheel hub.

Two church towers can be seen from this point. Coates parish church and Cirencester church.

Two of the Park's most striking buildings are within easy reach of Ten Rides. Three quarters of a mile along Broad ride are the Horse Guards, two ornamental arches resembling giant sentry boxes, while hidden in the woods to the left is Alfred's Hall, the first castellated folly, erected in 1732. Deliberately intended to resemble a ruin, this building contains ornamental features taken from Sapperton Hall, a nearby manor house bought and demolished by Earl Bathurst.

Dotted around the park are other decorative buildings, among them being Pope's Seat, the Round Tower, the Square House and the Hexagon.

Hailey Wood

Map 163, GR 966/066. Location sketchmap see page 102. Parking: Along Tunnel Inn approach track, off u/c Coates — Tarlton road.

This, the southernmost wood in Cirencester Park, appears the most remote and evocative of the wildwood of ancient times, yet is bisected by a railway and tunnelled under by a canal.

The railway, linking Stroud with Swindon, is still in use, but the canal, built to connect the Thames with the Severn (see page 124), has been derelict for many years.

Hailey Wood is best approached along the bumpy track leading from the Coates—Tarlton road to the Tunnel Inn. As the name suggests, this inn was built near the southern entrance to the Sapperton Tunnel and the restored portal can be viewed from the approach to the inn.

Close by, a public footpath sign denotes a way into the wood. The path eventually passes under the railway before swinging left along the line of the canal tunnel, the debris from which was dumped in the vicinity. This, together with old air shafts, account for the tree-covered mounds along the way.

Like Overley, Hailey is a mixed wood offering deer-spotting and bird-watching opportunities. In its south-west corner is the Star, a clearing from which eight rides radiate, one of which is Bath Ride, linking this point with Ten Rides in Oakley Wood.

Cotswold Water Park

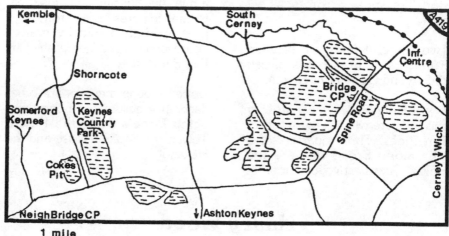

1 mile

The Cotswold Water Park is the all-embracing name given to an extensive complex of worked-out gravel pits in the Upper Thames Valley, bordering Gloucestershire and Wiltshire. Comprised of two distinct sections - one centred on the South Cerney, Somerford Keynes and Ashton Keynes area, the other around Fairford and Lechlade — the Park consists of 100 or so lakes covering almost 14,000 acres.

This is a man-made landscape — and a recent one at that. Apart from the digging of a canal to link the Thames with the Severn in the 1780s, and the construction of a railway link between Swindon and Cirencester a century later, this low-lying country between the Cotswolds and infant Thames was exclusively rural until the 1920s.

From that time onwards, gravel-extraction began to make an indelible impression on the tranquil scene. To begin with, the digging was confined to easily-worked gravel, and left shallow, uneven-bottomed pits which soon filled with water. Later, dragline excavators were introduced which dug deeper and extracted much greater quantities.

As demand increased, the detrimental effects of indiscriminate digging were at last recognised. Subsequent planning controls compelled the extractors to shelve the banks of the pits and to cover the land between with topsoil prior to landscaping.

More recently, a "dry" method of working has been practised. This involves pumping the water from

104

excavated areas to make total extraction and restoration easier. With the demand for gravel showing no sign of slackening, the likelihood is that by the end of the century, the Cotswold Water Park will become the largest concentration of man-made fresh water lakes in Britain.

The creation of an artificial "Lakeland" in the south Gloucestershire countryside has led to considerable interest being shown in the area's leisure and tourism potential. Naturalists, especially bird watchers, were quick to realise the value of such a vast extent of wetland habitat, as were the angling community. Devotees of a wide range of other water sports soon followed, and it was only a matter of time before a comprehensive recreational plan was conceived. This heralded the establishment of the Cotswold Water Park, a joint venture between the Gloucestershire and Wiltshire County Councils. The main access areas and the amenities they offer can be summarised as follows:

Keynes Country Park

Map 163, GR 027/957. Location sketchmap see page 104. Parking: Official car park (chargeable at peak periods) off u/c road between Spine Road and Shorncote.

Popular organised entertainment for the whole family — picnics, exercise trails and children's play areas. Toilets.

The gregariously inclined who like outdoor recreational facilities need seek no further. This is the Cotswold Water Park's Centre for country park fun with lakeside walks, picnic sites, barbecues, trimtrail, playground, children's beach, paddling area and nature reserve. Day tickets are available for angling and windsurfing.

Bridge Car Park

Map 163, GR 064/963. Location sketchmap see page 104. Parking: Official car park off Spine Road East.

Useful, easily-located starting point for exploring pools near South Cerney.

So named after the bridge beneath which until the 1960s the old railway linking Cricklade and Cirencester passed on its journey across a quiet landscape. The bridge is still preserved and on it a viewing platform has been built — an excellent idea — while beneath its brick arches, conservationists have fixed bat boxes in an attempt to prevent these fascinating, unjustly maligned animals from disappearing from our countryside.

From this small car park, the old railway line, now a footpath, can be followed either towards Cricklade or in the direction of South Cerney, passing a sailing lake on the left and two lakes on the right providing wildlife interest.

Neigh Bridge Country Park $| \oplus$

Map 163, GR 017/946.
Location sketchmap see page 104.
Parking: Official car park off u/c Somerford Keynes — Oaksey road.

Conveniently situated car park for exploring attractive Somerford

Keynes and the pools around its southern fringe.

A good starting point for a family exploration of the western section of the Water Park, offering picnic tables, a play area and short waterside walks. There are also angling opportunities.

Information Centre

Map 163, GR 072/972.
Location sketchmap see page 104.
Parking: First car park along Spine Road East from A419.

Unmanned centre making good starting point for walking the towpath of the Thames-Severn Canal.

The canal enters the Water Park at Northmoor Lane, north-east of South Cerney. Half a mile to the south is Boxwell Spring Lock, with a fall of only 3.5 feet, built in 1792 to enable water to be taken from nearby Boxwell Springs. Less than a mile south are the two Wildmoorway Locks, with falls of 7.5 feet and 11 feet re-

spectively. The lower of these two was fitted with a side-pond in 1831 to economise on water — always a problem on this waterway.

To the south of the Information Centre is the Cerney Wick Lock, with its distinctive tower-like round house, one of five built in 1790 alongside the 29 miles of waterway to provide clear views of the canal for the resident lock-keepers.

From the bridge near the round house, it is only a short distance to the village of Cerney Wick where refreshments can be obtained at the inn before the return walk.

Keynes Country Park Nature Reserve (Cokes Pit)

Map 163, GR 027/953. Location sketchmap see page 104. Parking: Off u/c Ashton Keynes — Shorncote road, half-a-mile E of Somerford Keynes.

8-acre nature reserve managed by GTNC.

Otherwise referred to as Lake 34 in the Water Park complex, this reserve is one of the oldest gravel pits in the Upper Thames Valley. It consists of a lake with several small islands, which provide suitable breeding sites for mute swan, great crested grebe, tufted duck, mallard and coot, as well as smaller waterside nesters such as reed buntings and sedge warblers. A hide enables good views of the birds to be had at close quarters.

There is a strip of flower-rich grassland along the lake's eastern margin and the dragonfly population includes the southern hawker, the black-tailed skimmer and the emperor.

Whelford Pools

Map 163, GR 174/995. Location sketchmap see page 104. Parking: Limited space off u/c Whelford — A417, SE of Fairford.

30-acre nature reserve managed by GTNC for the specialist naturalist.

This nature reserve consists of two flooded gravel pits separated by a narrow strip of land and there are two hides enabling visitors to see the extensive range of wildfowl that frequent the two sheets of water. This is an important reserve for wintering wildfowl, which are often deterred from using the other Water Park lakes through intense human activity. Duck species regularly visiting the pools during the winter months include mallard, pochard, wigeon and tufted duck, while such unusual visitors as red-crested pochard and ruddy duck have been recorded from time to time. In summer, the chief attractions are dragonflies, damselflies and a rich flora, both by the waterside and on the open dry ground between the pools.

Riverside Park, Lechlade ⊕

Map 163, GR 212/993.
Parking: Car park by A361,
S of Halfpenny Bridge,
Lechlade.

Flat, 20-acre grassy area a
good starting point for
walks into the town and
along the river bank.

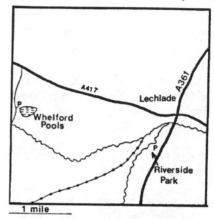

Lechlade is Gloucestershire's only Thames-side town and although the River Isis — as it is often called from here down to Oxford — is but a modest stream at this stage in its journey, it accounts for the 'messing about in boats' atmosphere that pervades the place. Three tributary rivers — Coln, Cole and Leach (from which the town gets its name) — swell the Thames nearby, while a mile upstream can be seen a round house built for the lock keeper of the 29-mile long Thames and Severn Canal (see page 124).

The extensive Riverside Park, serves as a suitable base from which to set off to explore the town and its environs. Lechlade may be a pleasure-boat haven today but its former prosperity was built on river — and later canal — trade. Farm products, especially cheeses, were loaded from its wharves for shipment to London, and a wander into its little square reveals something of this former importance.

Riverside walks can be taken in both directions from the park. Upstream, can be seen, as well as the canal round house, the mouth of the River Coln. Downstream, a delightful stroll awaits from Halfpenny Bridge (a toll bridge built in 1792), down to St. John's Lock. This is the highest lock on the river, alongside which can be seen Monti's statue of Father Thames, created for the Great Exhibition at the Crystal Palace in 1851.

Those wishing to return to the town (and Riverside Park) by a different route, can cross St. John's Bridge and turn left along a footpath just past the Trout Inn. This crosses fields to reach the town through the churchyard, along Shelley's Walk, so named because of the poet's affection for Lechlade. This he celebrated in a poem, the opening lines of which are reproduced on a commemorative stone nearby.

108

Cotswold Commons around Minchinhampton

Map 162.

A cluster of open commons with unrestricted public access, centred around the town of Minchinhampton.

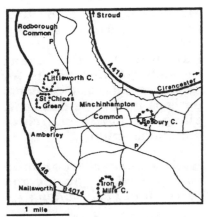

The area of the Cotswold plateau between Stroud and Nailsworth contains a considerable expanse of open common land, most of which is in the care of the National Trust or the county or local council, and offers unrestricted access to walkers. Although reduced greatly from their former 2000 acres extent, these commons provide invaluable space and freedom, with bracing air, fine views and varied wild life populations.

Old records show that this open downland was largely beech woodland until well into Saxon times. However, the Norman conquest saw a rapid reduction of the wooded area, as successive Ladies of the Manor (Abbesses of Syon) sold off the timber and encouraged the expansion of charcoal-burning to provide revenue for their estates. Despite the long-established commoners' rights, the local people were powerless to prevent the loss of their pannage (right to graze pigs) and estovers (right to gather fuel) as the woodlands continued to shrink. Fortu-

nately, however, the steep slopes and sparse soil of this terrain discouraged agricultural development, and the unimproved grassland and remnants of ancient 'waste' have become the unique leisure amenity and natural habitat we enjoy today.

The approach roads to some of these commons are extremely steep, narrow and tortuous, with passing places seemingly few and far between. Motorists should also note that cars should not be parked more than 15 yards from the road on such large commons as Rodborough and Selsley, and must on no account block approach roads or hinder commoners' access. Care should also be taken to keep dogs under control, especially when grazing livestock are present.

Minchinhampton Common

Map 162, GR 873/008.
Location sketchmap see page 109.
Parking: Of the many possible parking points for access to this vast common, perhaps the best is Bell Lane, along the parish church of Minchinhampton.

A 580-acre NT common widely used for grazing and recreation. Easy walking.

Second only in size to Cleeve Common, Minchinhampton Common, as distinct from the smaller commons scattered close by, is something of a crowd-puller. Throughout spring and summer, cars disgorge their passengers at every available parking space. This vast plateau, standing at 600 feet above sea level and offering as much fresh air as one could ask for, attracts walkers, picnickers, golfers, kite-flyers and riders from far afield.

Today's visitors are merely the latest in a long line of people who have found this area's lofty situation to their liking. We can still trace evidence of some of these long-departed settlers, for their earth-moving feats have left an indelible impression on this upland scene, in the shape of the Bulwarks.

These are a series of earthworks stretching in a rough, almost unbroken horseshoe for almost a mile and a half and enclosing roughly 200 acres of common. A theory has been advanced that they were constructed during the first half of the First Century AD by the British King Caractacus, as a defensive base against the invading Romans. Whatever their purpose, they add a welcome air of mystery to an exploration of this otherwise rather featureless common, and their potential for imaginative games will not be wasted on children.

Towards Amberley can be seen two more horseshoe-shaped ramparts, each extending for about three-quarters of a mile, which may be contemporary with the Bulwarks, or possibly of earlier origin.

What are without doubt much older, are the remains of a Neolithic long barrow known as Whitfield's Tump, on account of it having been used, in 1743, as a preaching platform by George Whitfield, one of the founders of Methodism. This can be seen close to the northern limit of the common, near the junction of the unfenced roads from Amberley and Minchinhampton.

On the westerly edge of the common at the junction of the lanes leading to Pinfarthings and

Theescombe, is the 18th century Rose Cottage, a distinctive three-storeyed house with pointed windows. It was here in 1852, that Dinah Mulock (later Mrs. Craik) wrote her novel 'John Halifax, Gentleman'. Although much of the story is set in Tewkesbury, Amberley appears as Enderley, and is described as 'Such a fresh, breezy spot — how the wind sweeps over it!'.

One other curiosity lies at the meeting place of six roads at the north-east of the common, where there is a multi-armed signpost known as Tom Long's Post. Who was Tom Long? Romantics cherish the belief that he was a highway man, who was captured (and some say hanged) at this cross-roads. Another often-told version is that Tom was a mere-footpad who, on being cornered, committed suicide here rather than face execution later. But perhaps the likeliest explanation is that the unfortunate Tom was a local labourer, who having taken his own life, was buried at the cross-roads in accordance with tradition.

Besbury Common

Map 162, GR 873/014. Location sketchmap see page 109. Parking: As for Minchinhampton Common (above).

A small hillside common, bisected by a minor road and with steep grassy scrambles for the more adventurous.

Best approached on foot across the Great Park, Minchinhampton, and along Besbury Lane. Besbury Common clings to the north-facing slope above the Golden Valley, a quiet hillside of humps and hollows and old anthills, crowned by an avenue of veteran beeches.

The wavy ribbon of road that wanders across it from Burleigh and Minchinhampton is called Love Lane and the faded, yet indelible pairs of initials that scar the weatherbeaten trunks of the old beeches may well be the handiwork of long-gone lovers. Their time, like ours today, would have been better spent admiring the view, which is truly magnificent.

Beyond the Golden Valley, snaking its sinuous way below, lies the heavily wooded coombe of the Toadsmoor Valley, its tiny stream cutting a miniature gorge as it delivers its waters into the River Frome. The story goes that the Golden Valley is so named, not on account of its beauty, but because the mills that lined the river in bygone times brought prosperity to their owners. Further wealth was generated by the coming of the Thames-Severn

Canal (see page 125), which led to the development of tiny Brimscombe glimpsed below to the left — into a busy inland port. The canal now lies derelict and the port's wharves and warehouses have gone, largely replaced by plastics factories, lying like scattered shoe-boxes cluttering the narrow valley below.

These pleasures include grassy slopes rich in wild flowers and ideal for picnics and play, a scatter of trees and bushes — ash, holly, field maple and more — providing shelter and variety of scene, and tempting footpaths leading past tucked-away cottages and farms to other secret places beneath the escarpment.

St. Chloe's Green & Littleworth Common

Map 162, GRs (St. Chloe's) 847/018, (Littleworth) 848/020. Location sketchmap see page 109. Parking: In Amberley village.

Two small, steep, undergrazed commons linked by public footpath.

These are two small commons north west of Amberley. Perched high above the Nailsworth Valley, they provide a sharp contrast with the wide expanse of Minchinhampton Common close by, for they are secret, well-wooded places, difficult to discover except on foot.

As they are linked by footpath, these little commons are best tackled by parking in the vicinity of Amberley War Memorial. From here, it is but a short step to St. Chloe's Green. The approach to the green is clearly indicated by the National Trust sign at a dip where two roads meet. Ashes, horse chestnuts and sycamores dominate the approach to

St. Chloe's Green. Soon however, the trees give way to a tangle of thorn and bramble, interspersed with patches of damp grassland which, in spring, is carpeted by a host of well-loved flowers. Violets, primroses and cowslips abound, as do salad burnet and, in good years, early purple orchid. Close by, sheltered by clumps of silver birch, wild garlic and bluebells hold sway, presenting an impression, albeit on a small scale, of the way much of this landscape must have appeared before the great clearance changed the upland scene for ever.

Approaching Littleworth Common along the footpath, the dominant feature is old hazel coppice, long since neglected and now essentially woodland. As elsewhere, building development has impinged a little of this north-west limit of the former vast common, but the scenic glimpses, the quiet, little-used paths and the ever-present wildlife provide interest along every step of the way.

Iron Mills Common, Ball's Green

Map 162, GR 865/995.
Location sketchmap see page 109.
Parking: On verge of u/c road off B4014, 1 mile E of Nailsworth.

Steep, grassy NT common with some scrub encroachment.

A small, steeply-sloping common, the southernmost of all those in the Minchinhampton area, Iron Mills overlooks the valley of the Nailsworth Stream or Little Avon, and Longford's Mill, which was built in the 18th century to produce high-quality cloth.

Despite its name, Iron Mills Common's chief claim to fame is its stone mine, securely fenced off now but with a tiny opening clearly visible. This was the so-called Upper Mine, first worked in the early 19th century and remaining operational until 1940.

This, together with Lower Mine, a short distance to the east, produced stone for the building of the Houses of Parliament. There are said to be 2000 yards of passages under the hillside, with galleries up to 30 feet high at the working face.

Fifty years later, it is hard to imagine the clamour of industry on this ancient common. A few oaks and beeches are dotted over the south-facing slopes, rising above the encroaching scrub. This aspect is favoured by meadow ants, which build their anthills over many years — up to 150 according to recent research. The brood chambers at the top of these mounds often attract green woodpeckers and badgers, the one using its long bill and sticky tongue to probe into the mounds, the other excavating much more deeply with its powerful front paws.

Rodborough Common | ⊕

Map 162, GR 857/036.
Location sketchmap see page 109.
Parking: Along unfenced road crossing common.

Grassy, NT common of 242 acres offering easy, bracing walking, with peripheral slopes offering challenging scrambles for the more energetic.

The most northerly of the cluster of commons standing high on the plateau south of Stroud, Rodborough is second only is size to Minchinhampton and, considering its close proximity to the bustling world of industry and commerce at its foot, is amazingly rural and remote.

Given to the National Trust in 1937, this fine common was in danger of losing its precious, uncluttered character to speculative builders. Some development had already taken place by then, including the sham castle known as Rodborough Fort, built to command the common's northern extremity in 1761, and rebuilt a century or so later.

The earliest evidence of human activity on Rodborough Common — two spear heads — have been dated as belonging to the Bronze Age, while some finely embossed bronze bands possibly represent the Dobunni people, who occupied the area in the century leading up to the Roman invasion.

But if historical interest is hard to come by on the wide expanse of Rodborough Common, the same cannot be said of the wild life. The lime-loving ground flora, in particular, is a constant source of delight throughout spring and summer. April sees the turf spangled with cowslips, early purple orchids and the tiny deep blue flowers of milkwort, while wood anemones, relics of the time when ancient woodland covered much of the common, cling on defiantly beneath the scattered scrubby hawthorns.

Summer brings a carpet of aromatic flowers to the grazed grassland. Wild thyme, marjoram and basil thyme thrive in these conditions and in turn attract a host of butterflies — meadow browns, marbled whites and common blues especially.

Two ground-nesting birds characterise high open commons such as Rodborough. Brown and unremarkable to the untrained eye, both skylark and meadow pipit keep the walker company over the springy turf.

Selsley Common

Map 162, GR 833/028. Location sketchmap see page 116. Parking: Numerous pull-ins along W side of B4066, S of Selsley.

Grazed hilltop common with easy access. Good views, flora and quarries with geological interest. Toilets.

Though often associated with Rodborough and Minchinhampton Commons, Selsley Common is separated from them by the valley of the Nailsworth Stream. Like Rodborough, it has a steep westerly-facing scarp, from the edge of which are superb views across the Severn estuary and, on clear days, far beyond, to encompass the Black Mountains of Wales.

Rising to 689 feet above sea level at its highest point, Selsley Common cannot fail to delight the seeker after wide open spaces. Striding briskly over the short turf, with the skylarks' ceaseless song cascading from above, the workaday world cluttering the valley below becomes an irrelevance.

From the northern end of the common, the eye falls upon the saddleback tower of All Saints' church, built in 1862 on the lower slopes of the scarp by the prominent Victorian architect G.F. Bodley. The style has been described as French Gothic, and the interior contains examples of the craftsmanship of several of the leading figures of the Raphaelite Brotherhood, including William Morris, Rossetti, Maddox Brown and Burne Jones.

Geologists, meanwhile, will be sure to find Leigh's quarry, at the southern end of the common, worth investigating (GR 826/025). The quarry face reveals beds of oolitic lower freestone, topped by softer oolitic marl, above which can be seen oolitic upper freestone. Nearer still to the surface are beds of fossiliferous material containing the remains of brachiopods and oysters.

Selsley Common also offers an archaeological site in the form of the Toots long barrow. All that remains of this ancient burial place (estimated date: 2900 BC) are two grassy mounds, the gap separating them originating possibly from early excavation, of which no record survives.

Those wishing to combine a visit to Selsley Common with a woodland stroll, should cross the stile into Pen Wood at the southern end of the common. The beeches in this scarp woodland are fine examples of this characteristic Cotswold tree.

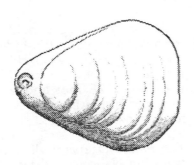
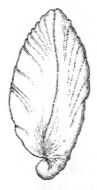

Brachiopod shell fossils

Coaley Park & Frocester Hill

Map 162, GR 795/015.
Parking: Coaley Peak picnic site and car park, off B4066.

Fine viewpoint plus walking and scrambling potential for the energetic. Information display. Toilets.

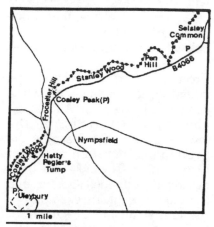

The OS map shows two viewpoints in close proximity just off the B4066 between Uley and Selsley Common. These vantage points are known as Coaley Peak (to the south) and Frocester Hill (to the north). Both hilltops take their names from villages at the foot of the scarp, and both, together with two Woodland Trust woods, Coaley Wood and Stanley Wood, can be reached along the Cotswold Way from the car park and picnic site, opposite the unclassified road to Nympsfield.

Glorious views over the Severn towards the Forest of Dean and the hills of Wales justify pulling off the road at this popular 13-acre site, created from a barley field and seeded to make two large paddocks. Minimum effort is needed to enjoy this superb vista.

Just beyond the car park is Nympsfield Long Barrow, a chambered burial mound dating from the Neolithic period (approx 2500 BC). This was first exca-vated in 1862, when it was found to contain thirteen skeletons, arranged in seated positions, together with pottery and a flint leaf arrowhead. Today, heavily restored after years of neglect, this ancient monument has lost much of its former impressiveness and it is hard to realize that until comparatively recent times, local people refused to approach it in the belief that it had been a leper's cell.

The nimble-footed should not miss walking along the escarpment edge to Frocester Hill nature reserve, where a topograph stands at 778 feet above sea level, complete with the distances to prominent landmarks.

The nature reserve itself, leased from the National Trust by the GTNC, comprises steep limestone grassland on which such attractive flowers as harebell, wild thyme, clustered bellflower and viper's bugloss persist despite intrusive bracken, bramble and scrub. The butterfly population includes the marbled white and common and holly blues, while as befits open upland terrain, skylarks and meadow pipits are characterstic bird species.

At the southern end of Frocester Hill can be seen a large abandoned quarry once valued by local builders for its high-quality freestone. Today, it affords ideal conditions for hartstongue fern, as well as such colonisers as ash and hawthorn, which need to be cleared on a regular basis.

Coaley Wood

Map 162, GR 794/004. Location sketchmap, see page 116.
Parking: Coaley Peak picnic site and car park (as above).

A 55-acre tract of scarp woodland, owned by the Woodland Trust and traversed by the Cotswold Way.

Extending southwards from Coaley Peak, Coaley Wood is another fine example of ancient broadleaved woodland, primarily beech and ash, beneath which grows a typical flora of dog's mer-

cury, wood anemone, sanicle and primrose.

On the woodland's eastern edge, though best reached directly from the B4066, stands an outstandingly well-preserved, 180 foot-long Neolithic chambered barrow known as Hetty Pegler's Tump. Fifteen skeletons were discovered inside during excavations in the mid-19th century. This monument is kept locked but the key may be obtained from a cottage further along the B4066 towards Uley. A torch and serviceable clothes are recommended.

Stanley Wood

Map 162, GR 794/015. Location sketchmap, see page 116.
Parking: Coaley Peak picnic site and car park (see above).

Steep, 93-acre Woodland Trust wood reached along

Cotswold Way. Care needed in wet conditions.

A mile-and-a-half of mixed woodland stretching along the Cotswold scarp slope, Stanley Wood links Pen Hill Woods with Coaley Peak and Frocester Hill, and provides some of the best woodland walking along the Cotswold Way.

The wood gets its name from the sprawling villages of Leonard Stanley and King's Stanley, which lie at the foot of the scarp, and from which numerous tracks and footpaths climb to it.

Gaps in the trees provide excellent views westward. Beyond the M5 and the Severn Vale, the Forest of Dean dominates the horizon, while away to the northwest, the Malverns rise with a majesty that belies their modest altitude.

Stanley Wood has had a chequered history. Formerly ancient beech and ash woodland, much of it was clear-felled in the 1950s and replanted with conifers. Thanks to natural regeneration however, the native trees had already begun to reclaim their own by the time the Woodland Trust purchased the wood and since then, a management programme intended to promote a return to the former broadleaved regime has ensured that Stanley Wood will not only retain its Cotswold character, but also its diverse ground flora.

This flora, together with three old limestone quarries, can be studied by leaving the Cotswold Way along some of the tempting side paths. But beware as the O.S. map indicates, the slopes are very steep and in places even the best in well-designed walking boots are put to the test!

Uleybury Hill Fort $\oplus$

Map 162, GR 784/989. Location sketchmap see page 116. Parking: Car park off B4066, N of Uley village.

Reasonably flat linear walking around ancient hill fort. Optional walks to Uley village by steep footpaths.

Nowhere in the south Cotswolds can we experience a greater sense of pre-history and scenic splendour combined than from the ramparts of Uley Bury, often described as one of the best examples of an Iron Age hill fort in the country.

The 13-acre central encampment is enclosed agricultural land and cannot be inspected, but by walking the four sides of this superb, roughly-rectangular promontory fort, dating from about 300 BC, we can begin to appreciate the degree of prowess the Iron Age inhabitants employed in constructing this defensive encampment. There were in fact three lines of defence — an inner bank, an upper terrace and bank, and a lower terrace, with entrances at the south, east and north corners.

Aerial photography has revealed that the interior area contained a series of small fields, ditches and circular dwellings, but as yet, no archaeological excavations within this area have been carried out.

Except at the north corner, Uley-bury must have been virtually impregnable, with steep drops of up to 300 feet all round. Those with boundless energy may well prefer to approach the fort from the village. In so doing, they will certainly appreciate the impressiveness of the setting, as well as gaining a sharper realisation of the true meaning of the word breathtaking.

Peaked Down and Cam Long Down

Map 162, GR 766/992.
Parking: Along u/c Dursley —
Coaley road, 1 m. NE
Dursley.

Steep ascents and bracing walking along footpaths over two privately-owned hills. Sweeping views in all directions.

Unlike the alluring slopes of Downham Hill away to the south, these two linked Cotswold outliers, nort-east of Dursley, can be climbed by public footpath. Peaked Down, better known as Cam Peak, is a conical hill with bracken-clad flanks. The ascent is short and steep, providing impressive views of the town of Dursley and its well-wooded surrounding countryside. In a depression on the summit is an iron frame, to which a cross is fastened at Easter-tide, when pilgrims from Cam and Dursley ascend the hill to celebrate Christ's Passion.

After crossing the ravine at Cam Peak's eastern extremity, the climb up to the Long Down's

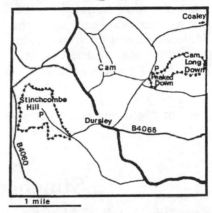

plateau-like summit is reasonably easy. Even so, the pitted surface should be crossed warily, as the numerous hollows resulting from a combination of earth-slips and quarrying are something of a hazard.

The views on both sides are richly absorbing. Looking north, the Severn Vale landscape is one of endless subtle variety — a patchwork of fields of every shape and size bordered by old hedges, many dotted with mature trees. A random scatter of villages and farmsteads completes the picture.

By contrast, to the south and east

119

are revealed the tree-clad eminences of the Cotswold escarpment — a sweep of fine upland country ranging from Breakheart Hill and the Ridge, above Waterley Bottom, to Bowcote Knoll and the great earthwork of Uley Bury.

Those wishing to vary their return route, and in so doing avoid scaling Cam Peak once more, should dip left by the ravine at the end of Long Down. At the foot of the slope, this route turns right to follow a sunken-way that skirts the Peak, running west from Hydegate to the stile on the Cotswold Way near Downhouse Farm.

Incidentally, Cam Peak may be a place of pilgrimage today but according to local legend, it owes its origin to the Devil. Determined to punish the people of Gloucestershire for building so many churches, Old Nick filled a wheelbarrow with Cotswold stone and set off one hot summer's day to dam the Severn and so drown the local population. On meeting a cobbler carrying several pairs of badly worn shoes, the perspiring Devil asked how far it was to the river. Suspecting the identity of his questioner, the cobbler, indicating the shoes, replied that it was so far distant that he had worn them all out through walking from there. Hearing this, the Devil, in disgust, tipped his load of stones at the foot of the Long Down — so giving rise to Cam Peak.

Stinchcombe Hill

Map 162, GR 745/984. Location sketchmap see page 119. Parking: Leave Dursley along May Lane, Hill Road and the Broadway. Pass golf clubhouse to reach small car park on left.

140 acres of Council-owned hilltop with magnificent views. Walking reasonably easy but with some steeper stretches and possible muddy patches.

Bustling, workaday Dursley nestles in the lee of Stinchcombe Hill and the golfers among its population justly claim that their hilltop course has the finest views of any in England.

From the car park, walk the few strides to the seat overlooking Hollow Combe. Have a list of superlatives ready — you will need them. To quote a travel book dated 1797: 'Stinchcomb Hill, near Dursley, commands prospects of as great extent and beauty as any eminence in the kingdom.'

The escarpment, clothed in dense woodland and crowned to the south by the Tyndale Monument, sweeps in a magnificent curve below. At the foot of the slope, a panorama of hedged fields fades away into the misty distance of the Severn Vale. To the right, Stinchcombe Hill's own wooded slopes thin out into patches of scrub as the vast spur swings out abruptly from the main scarpline to create the largest and most westerly of all the Cotswold hilltops, a rocky peninsula that in future geological time may join Cam Long Down, Robinswood, Churchdown and Bredon in the ranks of notable outliers of the main range.

In summer, the unimproved grassland between the golf greens and the beechwoods of the lower hill slope is carpeted with a rich variety of lime-loving wild flowers. Every step brings fresh rewards — wild thyme and rock rose, salad burnet and tiny chalk milkwort, hawkbit and carline thistle to name but a few. Here too, a tribe of grassland butterflies are active on sunny days — meadow brown, small heath and marbled white among the larger insects and common blue, brown argus and large skipper representing the smaller, more elusive species.

Taking the lower of two paths following the edge of the combe to the right, the view is one of subtle yet constant change. Below lies Stancombe Court, the country house from which the Clifford ladies of "Frampton Flora" fame, often sallied forth to draw the local wild flowers.

The scrub, though intrusive, is remarkably varied. Ash and pedun-culate oak are interspersed with dogwood, wayfaring tree, whitebeam and buckthorn. Clumps of birch are prominent in places, while such erratics as cotoneaster and holm oak — the latter being particularly persistent — stand out and require regular clearance to safeguard the vulnerable natural ground vegetation.

Drakestone Point, the south-west tip of Stinchcombe Hill, offers fresh views, impinged upon — some would say improved — by the works of man. From here, the M5 exerts its presence both visibly and audibly, while the Severn Bridge rears its proud geometry over the glinting Severn.

Swinging sharp right from Drakestone point, the path reaches the memorial seat to Sir Stanley Tubbs, who gave Stinchcombe Hill and its woods for the public enjoyment in 1930. Burgeoning woodland growth limits the scenic advantages of this seat today however, and it is best to press on to the topograph and triangulation pillar, standing at 719 feet above sea level. This offers superb views of the Severn Estuary, dominated in this stretch by Oldbury and Berkeley nuclear power stations and Sharpness Docks, backed by the dense wooded uniformity of the Forest of Dean.

Beyond a stone shelter, the route swings right along a bridleway and follows the boundary wall on the left before crossing between golf greens back to the car park.

Westridge Wood & Nibley Knoll ⊕

**Map 162, GR 757/943.
Parking: on verge of Old
London Road, 1 mile N of
Wotton-under-Edge.**

*Follow track signposted
Tyndale Monument.
Woodland and hilltop
walking along good tracks
and public footpaths,
including stretches of
Cotswold Way.*

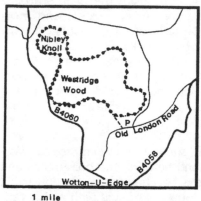

1 mile

Fine scenery, a wealth of wildlife
interest, and tangible traces of the
Cotswolds' historic past await the
walker on this splendid tract of
country north of Wotton-under-
Edge.

Westridge Wood is aptly named,
for it commands the high ground
over which the main road from
London once passed before
plunging down to the ancient little
town of Wotton. Formerly composed of native hardwoods, it is
now primarily larch plantations,
and there is no denying this deciduous conifer's grace of form and
colour, especially in its vivid
spring green and in the deep gold
of its autumn phase.

This is not to say that the beech,
ash and hazel coppice that once
clothed Westridge, have disappeared entirely. A search along
the steep, west-facing scarp soon
reveals a good number still surviv-

ing, especially in the vicinity of
Brackenbury Ditches, a well-sited,
triangular Iron Age hill-fort defended by two ramparts and covering some eight acres.

A short distance to the south-east,
close by the meeting of the approach lane with the Cotswold
Way at the woodland edge, is a
well-concealed old cockpit, a reminder of the barbaric sports that
flourished in rural areas in former
times.

Emerging from Westridge Wood,
the path sweeps boldly over the
close-cropped turf of Nibley Knoll
towards the Tyndale Monument,
passing a topograph overlooking
a varied pastoral landscape that
compels attention. From this
point, the eye travels in an arc encompassing the Severn bridge,
Haresfield Beacon, the nuclear
power stations of Oldbury and

Berkeley and, further west, the Sugar Loaf near Abergavenny. Here is the perfect spot to bring binoculars and absorb every subtle detail of this exceptional view, or alternatively, to let the spirits soar with a kite.

Tyndale's Monument, the tapering stone tower commanding this windswept ridge, was designed by the eminent Victorian architect S.S. Teulon and built in 1866. Rising to 111 feet, it was erected 'In grateful remembrance of William Tyndale, translator of the English Bible, who first caused the New Testament to be printed in the mother tongue of his countrymen'. Martyred for his faith in 1536, Tyndale is reputed to have been born in 1484 at North Nibley, nestling below the escarpment, and ranks among Gloucestershire's most famous men. Understandably, the tower is kept locked but the key can be obtained in the village.

The limestone pasture around the monument, together with the adjacent old quarry, provides a happy hunting ground for those to whom wild flowers and butterflies epitomise the finest treasures of the Cotswold uplands. Awaiting such visitors are the delights of early-purple orchid, rock rose, salad burnet and a legion of other colourful lime-loving blooms, attracting on sunny days common- and chalkhill-blues and large and small skippers.

Those who wish to picnic in the vicinity need look no further than the shady dell just beyond the monument.

Tyndale's Monument

Westonbirt Arboretum & Silk Wood | ⊕

Map 162, 850/900, off
A433, 4 miles SW of
Tetbury.
Parking: FC car park
(admission charge).

Westonbirt Arboretum :
Landscaped collection of
trees and shrubs covering
116 acres. Visitor centre,
exhibition, refreshments,
picnic area and toilets.
Limited disabled facilities.
Silk Wood: Large tract of
ancient oak woodland with
numerous rides and
avenues. Also new
plantings.

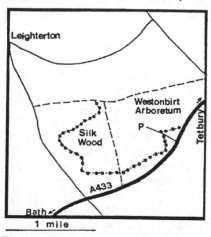

Westonbirt is the only location included in this book for which there is an admission charge. It is exceptional in every sense of the word. The largest arboretum in the country, its collection of maples is generally accepted as being the finest in the entire world. Together with adjacent Silk Wood, it contains over 15,000 specimens of temperate trees and shrubs set in 600 acres of semi-natural and landscaped woodland.

The arboretum was founded in 1829 by Robert Stayner Holford, of nearby Westonbirt House (now a school). He was succeeded by his son, Sir George Holford, and the family's devotion to Westonbirt continued through the fourth

Earl Morley, until 1956, when it was acquired by the Forestry Commission.

Whatever the season, Westonbirt provides a delightful day out. With seventeen miles of paths to choose from, it is usually possible, except at peak 'colour' weekends in autumn, to get away from the crowds. In spring, the main attractions are the displays of rhododendrons, azaleas, camellias and magnolias, together with the flowering cherries and bluebells, for which Silk Wood is noted. Summer sees the leaf mosaic at its greenest, with birds and butterflies adding their share of colour and interest.

The highlight of the Westonbirt year to many visitors is autumn, when the acers put on their almost breathtaking display of red, gold and yellow. There are leaves in plenty for the children to collect, while jays and grey squirrels are busy harvesting the acorn crop in Silk Wood.

Finally, a winter visit brings its own rewards. This is the time of year when the leafless trees can be studied in their unadorned splendour, with the woods and glades taking on a new appeal, yet hinting at the promise of the coming spring.

The independent-minded may choose to park off the A433, either at Willesley or Knockdown and follow the signposted bridle path through Silk Wood, returning along the unclassified lane from Leighterton. This is a pleasant enough walk in its own right, but is no substitute for paying the modest admission charge and enjoying the complete Westonbirt experience.

The Thames & Severn Canal

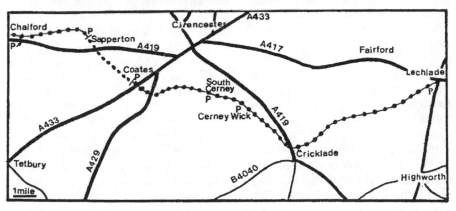

Map 163.
Parking: Lechlade, Riverside car park, GR 212/993, Cerney Wick, GR 960/079, Spine Road car park, South Cerney, GR 072/971, Tunnel House, Coates, GR 966/006, Daneway, Sapperton, GR 939/034, Valley Corner, Chalford, GR 903/025.

Starting points for walks along towpath of derelict canal. Approximately level throughout but subject to *mud and overgrowth according to season.*

A close scrutiny of OS Sheet 163 (Cheltenham and Cirencester) reveals the traces of an abandoned canal sweeping in a series of bold loops across almost the entire map.

The canal was the Thames and Severn, opened in 1789 which, in conjunction with the Stroudwater Canal, completed a decade earlier and linking Stroud with the

River Severn at Framilode, connected the country's two greatest rivers.

Those with an interest in industrial archaeology will no doubt want to follow the Thames and Severn Canal — both on the map and on the ground — from Chalford and westwards over OS Sheet 162 through Brimscombe to Stroud. As this four-mile section of the waterway passes through an industrialised, rather than a scenic landscape, we will concentrate here on the remaining 25 miles of the canal's course, sections of which feature elsewhere in the book under the headings Riverside park, Lechlade (page 108), Cotswold Water Park (page 104), Cirencester Park (page 100) and Siccaridge, Frampton and Sapperton Woods (page 99).

But first, something of the history of this ambitious waterway. Its construction entailed the building of 44 locks to carry it over the Cotswolds, as well as the digging of a 3,817-yard tunnel between Coates and Sapperton, passing beneath Cirencester Park. Despite the efforts of all involved in its construction, the Thames and Severn Canal was never completely successful. There was constant leakage at the summit level, a problem which was compounded by increasing competition from the railways.

Even so, statistics relating to the canal's early years make interesting reading; in 1841, for instance, a record 89,271 tons of freight was carried by the 70-foot horse-drawn narrow boats, comprising coal, limestone, iron ore, iron castings, textiles and dairy produce.

For a time too, the canal served in a passenger-carrying capacity. So-called 'fly boats' — lightweight vessels hauled by two horses — travelled at ten miles an hour or so along stretches of the waterway, and provided a far smoother ride than was possible along many of the turnpike roads.

By the beginning of the twentieth century however, the canal era was drawing to its close. The Thames and Severn was bought by the Great Western Railway and, despite several attempts to delay its closure, the end was inevitable. The Sapperton tunnel ceased to be passable after 1911 and the eastern section of the waterway was abandoned in 1927, to be followed by the remainder in 1933.

Over half a century of neglect later, canal enthusiasts still live in hope of restoring parts at least of the Thames and Severn to working order. The immensity of the task can be seen from any of the parking places listed above. For the general visitor, the most appealing features of the canal are the two tunnel portals and the three-mile stretch of towpath between Daneway and Valley Corner, Chalford.

River Access Points

WYE

Brockweir 539/012. Two-and-a-half mile riverbank walk N to Bigsweir.

Symonds Yat East 561/160. Mile-and-a-half riverside walk SW to Biblins along old railway track bed. Further if so desired.

SEVERN — WEST BANK

Bullo Pill 689/100. Small tidal creek — former shipbuilding site and port. Riverside walking.

Minsterworth 773/170. Riverside walks. Viewpoint for Severn bore. Interesting church and village.

Ashleworth 818/251. Riverside inn and walking. Fine church and tithe barn nearby.

Haw Bridge 844/278. Two riverside inns. Walks in both directions. South: to Maisemore via Ashleworth. North: to Tewkesbury via Chaceley Stock.

SEVERN — EAST BANK

Severn Way long-distance footpath — south from Tewkesbury to Shepardine. Good access points at: **Deerhurst** 868/298. Fine Saxon church and chapel. **Coal House Inn, Apperley** 855/283. Historic inn.

Upper Framilode 750/104. Junction of Stroudwater Canal and Severn.

Passage Inn, Arlingham 696/114. Old ferry point. Walks round peninsula.

COLN

Chedworth Roman Villa 055/135. One-and-a-half mile footpath E between river and woods to Yanworth Mill.

Coln Rogers 088/097. One mile walk upstream (N) to Calcot bridge.

Coln St. Aldwyns 143/047. Two mile walk upstream (W) to Bibury.

LEACH

The Eastleaches 202/053. Delightful villages with clapper bridge. One mile walk downstream (S) to Southrop.

WINDRUSH

Bourton-on-the-Water 168/207. Popular village with choice of riverside and lakeside walks.

Naunton 113/234. Pleasant village on Upper Windrush. Short riverside walks.

Taddington 086/312. One mile walk (S) along infant river to Cutsdean.

EYE

Upper Slaughter 155/233. Short walks N towards Eyford Park and S to **Lower Slaughter**, passing old water mill.

Long Distance Footpaths in Gloucestershire

Wye Valley Walk: S–N Chepstow — Ross 28 miles, Hereford 45. There is no more beautiful path in Britain, which follows the **west bank** of the River Wye. Signposting is excellent. Useful access points: Wynd Cliff GR 523/972, Whitebrook GR 538/068, Symonds Yat West GR 559/158, Stowfield GR 598/170, Kern Bridge GR 581/193. Also Chepstow, Tintern and Monmouth.

Offa's Dyke Path (Gloucestershire Section): S–N Chepstow — Monmouth, 12 miles. The Southernmost part of the Marches' most illustrious ancient way. It is clearly signposted along the **east bank** of the River Wye along the magnificent Wye Valley, and meets the Wye Valley Walk at Monmouth. Useful access points: Woodcroft GR 542/957, Brockweir GR 539/011, Bigsweir Bridge GR 539/051.

Severn Way Path: S–N Shepardine — Tewkesbury, 50 miles. A mixed route along the **east bank** of the wide Severn's panoramas. The route is signposted all along. Be wary of these flat-lands' notorious seasonal flooding and the effects of the Severn Bore (tidal surge), which together can make the path impassable. Useful access points: Sharpness GR 670/128, Frampton GR 750/080, Arlington GR 708/110, Haw Bridge (nr. Apperly) GR 845/279, Tewkesbury GR 888/326.

Cotswold Way: S–N Bath — Chipping Campden, 97 miles. Established in 1970, this frequently dramatic path follows the escarpment of the Cotswold Hills. Waymarking is excellent but long-distance walkers should use a printed guide from TICs. Useful access points: Stinchecombe Hill (nr. Dursley) GR 745/984, Coaley Peak GR 795/015, Painswick Beacon GR 868/118, Crickley Hill Country Park GR 928/163, Cleeve hill GR 986/270, Winchecombe GR 025/283, Hailes Abbey (nr. Winchecombe) GR 050/300, Dover's Hill (nr. Chipping Campden) GR 137/397.

Three other LDFs terminate within Gloucestershire. These are: the **Wychavon Way** at Winchcombe, which comes down from Holt Fleet nr. Worcester; the **Oxfordshire Way** at Bourton-on-the-Water, all the way from Henley-on-Thames; and the **Heart of England Way** at Chipping Campden. This 80 mile path connects the Cotswold Way with the Staffordshire Way further north. Most of these access points offer good parking facilities. Readers wishing to enjoy these LDFS to the full are recommended to consult page 134 for further material specific to the routes. Excellent guides are available from local TICs.

Additional Outdoor Attractions

FOREST OF DEAN
Puzzle Wood, Perrygrove Road, Coleford. One mile from Coleford on B4228. Wooded paths through old ironstone workings. Admission charge.

SEVERN VALE
Lydney Park Gardens, off A48, Lydney. Rhododendrons, azaleas and native spring flowers. Deer park. Admission charge.
Westbury Court, Water Garden, Westbury-on-Severn. Off A48. Rare formal Dutch-style water garden, laid out c. 1700. NT. Admission charge.
St. Augustine's Farm, Arlingham. Off A38. 124-acre working farm on peninsula by River Severn. Farm trail.
Wildfowl and Wetland Trust, Slimbridge. Off A38. 800 acres of wetland with waterfowl collection and hides for viewing estuary birds. Admission charge.

COTSWOLDS
Hidcote Manor Gardens, near Mickleton. Off B4632. Superb plant collection. NT. Admission charge.
Kiftsgate Court Gardens, near Mickleton. Off B4632. Delightfully situated gardens. Admission charge.
Batsford Park Arboretum, near Moreton-in-Marsh. Off A44. 50 acres of species-rich woodland. Admission charge.
Broadway Tower Country Park. Off A44 near Broadway. 37 acres of woods and grassland, with observation tower. Admission charge.
Cotswold Farm Park. Off B4077, near Guiting Power. Unique collection of rare livestock breeds. Admission charge.
Folly Farm, Bourton-on-the-Water. Off A436. Extensive waterfowl collection. Admission charge.
Denfurlong Farm Trail. Off A429, near Chedworth. Two farm trails showing land forms, crops and livestock.

GUIDED WALKS
Forest of Dean: Timewalk, Sling, Coleford (0594-33544).
Cotswold: Cotswold Warden Service, County Planning Dept. Glos. County Council, Shire Hall, Gloucester (0452-425674).

Index of Places

GLOUCESTERSHIRE
Discover the Countryside

Gloucestershire County Council is justly proud of the beautiful countryside in the county it helps administer, and is involved with many different agencies to ensure that it is well looked after and that the beauty remains. Close, regular links are maintained with the Forestry Commission, the Farming and Wildlife Advisory Group, the Gloucestershire Trust for Nature Conservation, the National Trust and the Countryside Commission (to name but a few) in order to protect the glorious natural heritage of Gloucestershire. The County Planning Department own and care for seven sites, five on the Cotswolds and two in the Cotswold Water Park and conservation has a high priority in site management plans. The department also administers the Cotswold Warden Service who care for 765 square miles of the Cotswolds Area of Outstanding Natural Beauty, over 60% of which is in Gloucestershire.

However, the emphasis is not just on preservation but also in enjoyment. The County Council wants to help people enjoy the countryside and to treasure it, by understanding how it works and by exploring it in ways that will preserve its harmony. The Discover the Countryside campaign, set up in 1990, helps achieve this by providing information in a variety of interesting ways.

There are a number of **Fact Sheets** available from the address below which cover the following subjects:

Activity Breaks	Arts & Crafts Attractions
Attractions Open All Year	Attractions Accessible to Disabled People
Country Churches	Country Parks Picnic Sites & Access Areas
Farm Food & Produce	Forestry Commission Properties
Farms Open to the Public	Industrial Heritage Attractions
Gardens & Arboreta	National Trust Properties
Historical Interest Attractions	Walking in the Cotswolds
Museums in the Countryside	Walking in the Forest of Dean
Wildlife Attractions	Walking in the Severn Vale

Information is also available for Accommodation, Camping & Caravanning, Cycling and Public Transport.

For any of these publications or for further advice and guidance contact:
Countryside Information Service,
County Planning Department, Shire Hall, Gloucester GL1 2TN
Telephone: 0452 425673

Recommended Reading and References

Books — background information

Ordnance Survey. The Cotswolds. Landranger Guidebook.
Ordnance Survey. Leisure Guide. Cotswolds.
Ordnance Survey. Leisure Guide. Forest of Dean and Wye Valley.
Severn Tide. Brian Waters. Alan Sutton.
The Forest of Dean. Humphrey Phelps. Alan Sutton.
Cleeve Hill. The History of the Common and its People. David H.Aldred.
       Alan Sutton.
Gloucestershire's Green Heritage. Mary Hopkins. Barn Owl Books.
Nature Reserves Handbook. GTNC.

Books — walking guides

Theme Walks in Gloucestershire. Gordon Ottewell. Thornhill Press.
The Cotswold Way. Mark Richards. Penguin.
A Guide to the Cotswold Way. Richard Sale. Constable.
Family Walks in the Cotswolds. Gordon Ottewell. Scarthin Books.
Family Walks in South Gloucestershire. Gordon Ottewell. Scarthin Books.
Cotswold Walks Pathfinder Guide. Ordnance Survey.
Wildlife Walkabouts: South Cotswolds & North Avon. Rosemary Teverson.
       Wayside Books.
Wildlife Walks in the North Cotswolds. Gordon Ottewell. Thornhill Press.
The Severn Way Path (East Bank). S. Gidman. Glos. County Library

Booklets, leaflets, etc.

Daffodil Way. Windcross Public Paths Project.
Poets' Paths 1 and 2. Windcross Public Paths Project.
Crickley Hill: Village, fortress, shrine. Richard Savage.
Cotswold Way Handbook. Ramblers' Association.
Forest of Dean Heritage Guides. Published jointly by the Dean Heritage
       Museum and Forestry Commission

Log Cabin,
Symonds Yat

Tourist Information Centres

The value of TICs, as they are popularly known by those of us who enjoy discovering the remoter places of the countryside, cannot be over emphasised. They are all staffed by locals who, if they have no personal experience of the place that interests you, will provide a good information source. Do not make the mistake of assuming TICs to be nothing but B&B agencies. Gloucestershire TICs may be found in two forms: Grade One is open throughout the year, offers county-wide bed-booking and has a full range of information; Grade Two is located in smaller towns and offers services restricted to their immediate vicinity, and some close in winter.

GRADE ONE

Cheltenham Spa: Municipal Offices, The Promenade. Tel: (0242) 522878.
Cirencester: Corn Hall, Market Place. Tel: (0285) 654180.
Coleford: Council Offices. Tel: (0594) 366307.
Gloucester: St. Michael's Tower, The Cross. Tel: (0452) 421188.
Stow-on-the-Wold: Talbot Court, off Sheep Street. Tel: (0451) 31082.
Stroud: Subscription Rooms, Kendrick Street. Tel: (0453) 765768.
Tewkesbury: Information Office, The Museum, Barton Street. Tel: (0684) 295027.

GRADE TWO

Cinderford: The Library, Belle Vue Road. Tel: (0594) 22581.
Chipping Campden:* Woolstapler's Hall Museum, High Street. Tel: (0386) 840289.
Newent: Newent Library, High Street. Tel: (0531) 822145.
Northleach:* Cotswold Countryside Collection. Tel: (0451) 60715.
Painswick: The Library, Stroud Road. Tel: (0452) 812569.
Tetbury:* Old Court House, Long Street. Tel: (0666) 503552.
Winchcombe:* The Town Hall, High Street. Tel: (0242) 602925.
* Seasonal opening only.

Ramblers Association

The Ramblers' Association exists to pursue four main aims: to promote rambling, to protect footpaths, to seek public access to open country and to defend the natural beauty of the countryside. Set up in 1935, the association has a large membership and more than 330 local RA groups. Members receive copies of the association's quarterly colour magazine and our annual Rambler's Yearbook and Accommodation Guide. In addition, they may borrow OS maps from our extensive library and are eligible for discounts in certain outdoor equipment stores.

Local groups organise regular programmes of walks as well as practical footpath work and social evenings. To campaign with even greater success, we need to increase our membership so that we are seen to be truly representative of all those who love rambling in the countryside.

For more information, please contact:
The Ramblers' Association,
1–5 Wandsworth Road,
London SW8 2XX.
Telephone: 071 582 6878.

Open Spaces Society

The Open Spaces Society, formally the Commons, Open Spaces and Footpaths Preservation Society, was founded in 1865 and is Britain's oldest national conservation body. We campaign to protect common land, village greens, open spaces and public paths and your right to enjoy them. We advise local authorities and the public on common land and public path law, and give support to campaigns on a local level.

Members have instant access to the society's advisory service; receive the society's informative journal three times a year and are entitled to discount on the society's publications. For more information please contact:
The Open Spaces Society,
25a Bell Street,
Henley on Thames,
Oxon RG9 2BA.
Telephone: (0491) 573535.
(Registered charity no. 214753).

For Lottie Stroud, a fine teacher and true friend.

About the Author

A native of Derbyshire, Gordon Ottewell worked in the coalmining industry for ten years before becoming a teacher. He served as a Primary Head in schools in Oxfordshire and Gloucestershire before taking early retirement in 1988. As well as being the author of several books on countryside exploration, he has been responsible for the 'In the Country' and 'Rural Rides' features in the 'Gloucesterhire Echo' for many years and also writes the monthly 'Wold Walk' feature in 'Cotswold Life' magazine. He is well known in Gloucestershire and neighbouring counties as a speaker on countryside matters and has broadcast frequently on local radio.

Notes

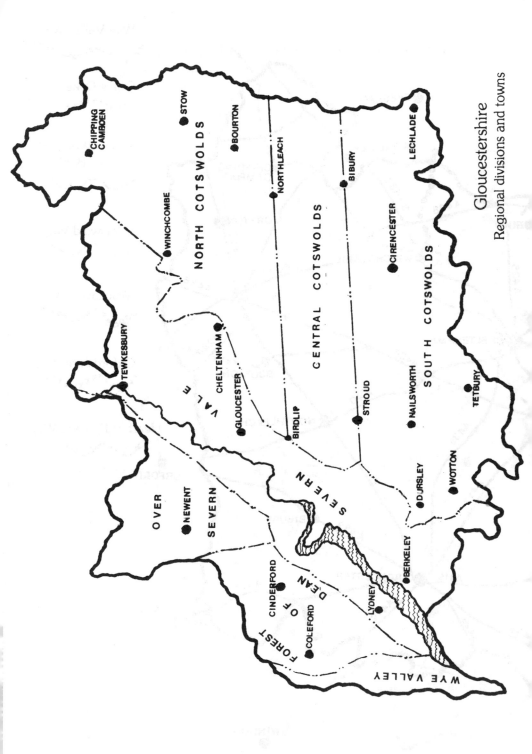

Gloucestershire
Regional divisions and towns